IKE
1890-1990
A PICTORIAL HISTORY

Also by Douglas Kinnard

The Secretary of Defense (1980)

The War Managers (1985)

President Eisenhower & Strategy Management:
  A Study in Defense Politics (1989)

An AUSA Book

An AFA Book

IKE 1890-1990

A PICTORIAL HISTORY

DOUGLAS KINNARD

Wade Tyree, *Photo Editor*

 BRASSEY'S (US), Inc.
Maxwell Macmillan Pergamon Publishing Corp.

Washington · New York · London · Oxford
Beijing · Frankfurt · São Paulo · Sydney · Tokyo · Toronto

Book Design and Production by
Yaron Fidler

Brassey's (US), Inc.

Editorial Offices   *Order Department*
Brassey's (US), Inc.   Macmillan Publishing Co.
8000 Westpark Drive, 1st Floor   Front and Brown Streets
McLean, VA 22102   Riverside, NJ 08075

Brassey's (US), Inc., books are available at special discounts for bulk
purchases for sales promotions, premiums, fund-raising, or educational use through the Special Sales Director, Macmillan Publishing
Company, 866 Third Avenue, New York, New York 10022.

Library of Congress Cataloging-in-Publication Data
Kinnard, Douglas.
Ike 1890–1990 : a pictorial history / Douglas Kinnard.
p.   cm. — (An AUSA book.)
"An AFA book."
ISBN 0-08-037445-X
1. Eisenhower, Dwight D. (Dwight David), 1890–1969—Pictorial
works. 2. Presidents—United States—Biography—Pictorial works. 3.
Generals—United States—Biography—Pictorial works. 4. United
States. Army—Biography—Pictorial works. I. Title. II. Series: AUSA
Institute of Land Warfare book.
E836.K56 1990
973.92'092—dc20
[B]   89-77568
                                                               CIP

Published in the United States of America

Foreword

It is a special pleasure to join in this anniversary tribute to a distinguished American leader, Dwight David Eisenhower. Ike was very important to each of us. Two of us served with him in World War II and one of us worked with him daily in close political cooperation. He was the commander in chief to one of us and, even after his presidency, we were privileged to have his advice on important issues. To all, he was a man eminently worthy of this commemorative volume.

In so many ways, Ike was the epitome of the American dream—rising from humble beginnings in a small farming community in the Midwest, to the victorious leadership of the greatest army ever assembled, and on to the presidency while America dealt with grave international challenges and control of the thermonuclear genie. Following the trauma of World War II and the Korean War, President Eisenhower's eight years in office are now remembered as extraordinarily peaceful and stable.

Eisenhower's legacy still lives, and *Ike 1890-1990* is one of the fitting tributes that will be paid to this unique man during the commemorative year. We are pleased to join this salute to Ike.

Gerald R. Ford

Jimmy Carter

Ronald Reagan

A Special Tribute

In 1945, at a ceremony in the historic Guildhall in London, General Eisenhower said, "I come from the heart of America." In 1990, as we celebrate the centennial of his birth and the forty-fifth anniversary of the end of the Second World War, those who live in the heart of Europe are daring to breathe free after living for generations under tyranny. For a man who led the greatest expeditionary force in history to free Europe from another kind of tyranny—a man who dedicated his life to preserving and protecting the ideal of freedom that dwells in the heart of America—there could be no greater tribute.

Dwight David Eisenhower's achievements made him one of our greatest generals and greatest presidents. But perhaps an even greater legacy than his achievements as a leader is what we remember about Eisenhower as a man. After the millions of words that have been written and spoken about him in the twenty-one years since his death, no one has said it more eloquently than he did himself to Mamie a few hours before he died. "I have always loved my wife," he said. "I have always loved my children. I have always loved my grandchildren. And I have always loved my country."

As one who had the privilege of serving as his vice president during the time when he consolidated in peacetime the triumphs for freedom that he had won in war, I commend the author and publishers for this new pictorial history of his life. It will permit new generations of Americans to learn and marvel at what one man—one extraordinary man—can do.

An AUSA Institute of Land Warfare Book

The Association of the United States Army, or AUSA, was founded in 1950 as a not-for-profit organization dedicated to education concerning the role of the U.S. Army, to providing material for military professional development, and to the promotion of proper recognition and appreciation of the profession of arms. Its constituencies include those who serve in the Army today, including Army National Guard, Army Reserve, and Army civilians, and the retirees and veterans who have served in the past, and all their families. A large number of public-minded citizens and business leaders are also an important constituency. The Association seeks to educate the public, elected and appointed officials, and leaders of defense industry on crucial issues involving the adequacy of our national defense, particularly those issues affecting land warfare.

In 1988 AUSA established within its existing organization a new entity known as the Institute of Land Warfare. Its purpose is to extend the educational work of AUSA by sponsoring scholarly publications, to include books, monographs, and essays on key defense issues, as well as workshops and symposia. Among the volumes chosen for designation as "An AUSA Institute of Land Warfare Book" are both new texts and reprints of titles of enduring value that are no longer in print. Topics include history, policy issues, strategy, and tactics. Publication as an AUSA Book does not indicate that the Association of the United States Army and the publisher agree with everything in the book, but does suggest that the AUSA and the publisher believe this book will stimulate the thinking of AUSA members and others concerned about important issues.

An AFA/AEF Book

The Air Force Association (AFA), established on February 6, 1946, is an independent veterans' organization whose objective is to promote greater understanding of aerospace and national defense issues. On May 1, 1956, AFA established the Aerospace Education Foundation (AEF). The Foundation was established as a nonprofit organization in order to formulate and administer AFA's educational outreach programs.

With a membership of more than 240,000, AFA represents all elements of the Air Force family, military and civilian, active and retired, Reserve and National Guard, cadet and veteran, Civil Air Patrol, civil service, and aerospace workers.

Brassey's AFA Book Series is designed to assist AFA's Aerospace Education Foundation in fulfilling its mandate. AEF's goal is to inform AFA members—and indeed anyone involved in the national defense dialogue—about issues vital to the future of the U.S. Air Force in particular and air power in general. Forthcoming AFA Books may cover the topics of aerospace history, biography, technology, combat, strategy and tactics, personnel, management, leadership, and policy. Publication as an AFA Book does not indicate that the Air Force Association and the publisher agree with everything in the book, but does suggest that the AFA and the publisher believe this book will stimulate the thinking of AFA members and others concerned about important issues.

Contents

CHAPTER 1

Ike and His Times

Gettysburg was more than a refuge for him. While Ike was president Bruce Catton wrote, "Then the perplexing mists and shadows would fade and Gettysburg would reveal itself as a great height from which men could glimpse a vista extending far into the undiscovered future." Gettysburg was a colossal reminder right out of U.S. history, an inescapable warning about what we Americans could inflict on each other, never mind what a foreign enemy could do. Dwight Eisenhower had that sense of history. It had been fostered under the tutelage of General Fox Conner as the two of them rode horses through the jungles and hills of Panama in those sad, frustrating days after World War I. Then Ike had slipped backward from lieutenant colonel down to major and then further down to captain again, leaving him to wonder if he'd ever do better than coach football on Army posts and to try to understand why life had been denied to "Icky," the baby Dwight David Junior.

The Eisenhower family line stretched from the Kansas prairie town of Abilene back to Germany via the Pennsylvania countryside that Ike would later seek as his sanctuary. In 1911 the talented high school athlete who played football and fielded for both his high school and a semiprofessional baseball team would go against the grain of his Mennonite family's religious beliefs to attend the United States Military Academy for its free education and athletic opportunities. But here he would endure his first great disappointment: two weeks before the 1912 Army-Navy game, he damaged his knee in a game with the Jim Thorpe–led Carlisle (Pennsylvania) team. Unwisely, he played again the following week in a game against Tufts, where he so injured his knee that he was forced to give up football. His athletic horizons—his *raison d'être*—were so limited now that he contemplated quitting the Military Academy. But he pursued his studies in stoic acceptance of his fate.

While West Point failed to stimulate the small-town boy from Kansas, his naturally bright mind was later awakened by General Fox Conner who encouraged Ike to read and stretch his mind. In 1925 he went to the hypercompetitive Command and General Staff School where Army careers were made or unmade and where failures, even mediocre performances, sometimes led to suicides. Conner believed a second world war loomed ahead and confidently saw the potential of Ike and that of another officer, a major named George C. Marshall. Ike went to the Leavenworth school and graduated first in a class of 275.

But despite his ambivalence about his West Point experience, Eisenhower always kept a watchful eye on the academy and was ever willing to fine-tune its formula. After World War II, he came back from Europe as Army chief of staff and advised the Military Academy's new superintendent, General Maxwell Taylor, to improve the West Point honor system and to institute formal classroom training in military leadership. As Taylor and his staff sought incrementally to modernize the cadet experience, Eisenhower gave them an additional suggestion: "Don't make West Point unreachable for a kid from Abilene High School." He had wanted to escape from Abilene as a young man and he wasn't 100 percent enamoured of West Point, but he never forgot either one.

Ike would labor in the peacetime "Brown Shoe Army"—the army in the years between the world wars where promotion and career satisfaction were rare commodities. He would serve under General Douglas MacArthur twice, first while MacArthur was Army chief of staff and later in the thirties in the Philippines. Stateside again with the war in Europe already raging, more preparations had to be made for what the prescient saw as inevitable. In the great Louisiana field maneuvers in 1941, an obscure temporary brigadier general named Eisenhower showed he had learned his lessons so well that the new Army Chief of Staff George C. Marshall jumped Ike over several hundred, shocked, senior generals to eventual command of the North African campaign Torch.

Ike had a temper all his life. He could try to emulate his boss Marshall who would preside over all the chaos around him and maintain an unshakable poise that others would marvel at, but Eisenhower couldn't muster Marshall's Olympian calm. Ike struggled with his temper, trying to hold it in check. But it appeared anyway, through Torch, Husky, Avalanche, and Overlord, the great campaigns of World War II. Still he handled himself superbly, even when his generals would bicker among themselves, stepping on each other's toes, grabbing for resources and jockeying for commands, demanding more planes, guns, supplies, and men, fighting with each other for attention like children already given too much. Ike often confronted the most frightening "enemy" in his own headquarters and billets: the all-too-human faces and delicate emotions of the subordinates who were part of his ever-growing responsibilities.

He made choices and lived as well as he could with their consequences. And the decisions were tough, involving the lives of many men. Before the Husky invasion of Sicily, the first step to regain the European continent, Allied code breakers cracked the German Enigma cryptographic system, revealing to Allied headquarters that the lightly armed paratroopers of the U.S. Army's 505th Regiment would be confronting the heavily armed Tiger tanks of the Hermann Göring Panzer Division. Eisenhower chose not to inform his paratroopers beforehand; if they were captured and revealed their prior knowledge of the German's Sicilian defense, the Germans would find out that their codes had been cracked.

Rank had its privileges for Ike, but he wore it lightly, realizing that wars were won by individuals working together and everyone's contribution had to be recognized whenever possible. Less than a week after the Husky invasion started, Ike made a sea journey aboard the British destroyer HMS *Petard* to view the progress of the invasion. The destroyer came under artillery attack from a German shore battery, Ike's first time under actual combat fire in his career, though he was a four-star general by then. Later he and an entourage landed at Correnti where Canadian units held a quiet beachhead. Ike and his group had been brought from the ship to the beach on a duck, an amphibious truck, and he was the first off onto terra firma. A British officer was standing nearby and Ike went to him and said, "Good morning. I am General Eisenhower." The Britisher was shocked speechless. Ike continued, "I want to talk with the senior Canadian officer on this beachhead."

The Britisher regained his composure and advised, "This is the Canadian beachhead, sir; headquarters are some distance inland."

Eisenhower insisted, "I don't care if it's a second lieutenant, but I want to meet some Canadian officer. I have come to welcome Canada to the Allied command."

He oversaw the invasion of the Italian mainland and then waited tensely in the violent wind and rains of early June 1944 for his weathermen to approve the monumental cross-Channel invasion of France. When the war ended, he expressed his gratitude to the Allies who had sometimes fought their own battles with him. He told the British:

> Five years and eight months of war, much of it on the actual battleline, blitzes big and little, flying V-bombs—all of them you took in your stride. You worked, and from your needed efforts you would not be deterred. You carried on, and from your midst arose no cry for mercy, no wait of defeat.

Eisenhower was the last of a group of five generals who

distinguished themselves in war to such an extent that the voters irresistibly gave each the presidency—George Washington, Andrew Jackson, Zachary Taylor, Ulysses S. Grant, and Eisenhower.

He left the Army early in the summer of 1952 to campaign for the Republican presidential nomination.. He was a relative latecomer into the field, when today we suffer contemporary presidential campaigns with all their speeches, fund-raising, posturing, and "no comment" answers beginning years before the first primaries. Now it seems that Ike had been waiting in the wings for the presidency since V-E Day in 1945. To his credit and in contrast to modern presidential aspirants, he kept to whatever business was at hand—Army chief of staff, president of Columbia University, and NATO commander. He beat Senator Robert Taft of Ohio for the nomination in July 1952 on the first ballot and went on to defeat the cerebral Democratic candidate Governor Adlai Stevenson of Illinois in November: thirty-four million popular votes to twenty-seven million and 442 electoral votes to 89. Four years later he faced Stevenson again and clobbered him even more decisively: thirty-six million popular votes to twenty-six million; 457 electoral votes to 73.

Ike was a professional soldier long before he was a practicing politician. Necessity had dictated learning political lessons—lessons begun with his observations as a staff officer and with those readings General Conner assigned in Panama. And he kept learning as he rose up the ladder. In 1932 he warned Chief of Staff Douglas MacArthur to avoid appearing with the Army troops when they attacked protesting, impoverished World War I veterans camping in tarpaper shacks at Anacostia Flats in Washington during the worst of the Great Depression. MacArthur went anyway to command at the scene as his troops attacked the "mob," as MacArthur called them. Major Eisenhower dutifully went along and stood at MacArthur's side that night. After police officers fatally shot two veterans, the Army forces attacked with fixed bayonets, and the veterans' shantytown was torched. A photo shows Ike standing next to MacArthur. The major looks impassive while the general mops his brow, but the lesson couldn't have been lost on Ike. Like Gettysburg, it reminded him of what people were capable of doing to each other.

As a professional soldier, Ike could accept that all the resources and all the planning never guaranteed a successful outcome; there were unpredictable intangibles that Carl von Clausewitz, the great German martial philosopher of the nineteenth century, called "friction." Usually these frictions were of a human element. As a professional-soldier-turned-politician, Dwight Eisenhower had the soldier's healthy sense of pragmatism. Great goals could be set, but they had to be set with a measure of realistic expectations. Ike was able to ameliorate others' human foibles such as MacArthur's posturing at Anacostia, George Patton's slapping the hospitalized soldier in Sicily, Charles de Gaulle's haughtiness, Patton's squabbling with Bernard Montgomery, Matthew Ridgway's fighting with Boy Browning, Richard Nixon's fragility before the Checkers' speech, and his own presidential aide Sherman Adams undoing himself by accepting an expensive vicuña coat as a gift.

Eisenhower did make decisions he later regretted. As president, he appointed Governor Earl Warren chief justice of the Supreme Court, believing the Californian was a predictable, pragmatic politician who wouldn't upset any apple carts. Instead, Warren painfully surprised Eisenhower by leading the Supreme Court into revolutionizing American law in civil liberties and the rights of accused criminals. The actions inspired outrage at Ike's choice and fomented legal controversies lasting well into the following decades.

Ike saw brushfire wars fed by revolutionary impatience and brinksmanship grow to such intensity that they threatened to ignite international forests. He watched India pass from a British colony into fragile nationhood and be consumed by the mutually antagonistic forces of Mahatma Gandhi's civil disobedience and the violence between Hindus and Muslims. In the Near East, those Jews who had witnessed or survived the sheer horror of Hitler's hate and its brutal mechanics would wait no longer for British indulgence in Palestine. So the long-prayed-for Jewish homeland came to be with the establishment of the modern state of Israel. The conflicts between Israelis and their Arab neighbors have rarely abated since and later directly concerned Eisenhower himself in the Suez Crisis of 1956.

He would inherit the stalemate of Korea and see the finale of French colonialism in Indochina in 1954 that seduced him into believing it was America's turn to exert a regional influence. In Africa, too, the growing chorus for national independence sang louder while more brushfire wars continued in Algeria and flamed in the Congo.

But he saw more than changes wrought by war. He also saw many extraordinary advances during the preciously short, peaceful periods that the United States was blessed with occasionally. In 1911 he had journeyed by train from Abilene to enroll at West Point; that trip nearly halfway across the country required several days to complete. As president, he initiated the most extensive road building project the United States has ever seen—the interstate highway system, which now allows motorists to span the continent in less than 60 hours. During Ike's youth, daring adventurers struggled to get their rickety aircraft inventions off the ground. By the end of his presidency, a new passenger jet, the Boeing 707, could fly over the entire continent in a few hours. Late in his presidency, the Russians would shatter our belief in U.S. technological and industrial superiority by sending men into space and orbiting our planet. It may have pained him to take second place in the race for space then, yet the feat was something to marvel at nonetheless. Medical marvels were achieved as well. All through Ike's life, parents feared their children would be crippled or even die from polio. The death of a beloved child was something Ike knew only too well. Dr. Jonas Salk's invention in the early fifties of a vaccine to prevent polio was surely an immense achievement in Ike's eyes.

In World War II, mysterious electronic machines took the jumbled letters and words of enemy codes and put them into understandable language so Ike and his men could better glimpse their enemies' intentions. During his presidency, these computers would work more wonders. Another electronic invention would simultaneously allow moving pictures and sound in everyone's parlors at the same time the action was taking place. The widespread use of television in American households began in Eisenhower's first administration. The same electronics helped create a new music and culture, almost tribal, that many said wouldn't last. It was called "rock and roll." Later, after his presidency and after the tragic murder of his successor John F. Kennedy, that new culture and music would influence a war.

Ike was unique among his famous contemporaries. His face more often expressed his feelings than it masked them, though he could muster appropriate reserve when necessary. He could never have emulated Franklin Delano Roosevelt's patrician jocularity or the characteristics of his other contemporaries: the tenaciousness of Winston Churchill, the consuming pride of Douglas MacArthur, the near-arrogance of Charles de Gaulle, the cold calculation of Joseph Stalin, the puckish energy of Harry S Truman. Eisenhower's expressions ran a wider spectrum of emotions, giving him a refreshing "uncommon commonness."

There is the child, a fifth-grader dressed in overalls at Abilene's Lincoln School, slightly scared by the camera, his hands holding his cap as a shield in front of him. Several years later and still in overalls, an adolescent Ike on a camping trip smiles with a little mischief, like Huck Finn, his hands still in front. Seated in the front row of his Abilene High School baseball team, arms folded in his lap, he tilts his head, seriously considering the camera as a diamond opponent. He is tight-lipped and slightly apprehensive on a Chicago street en route to West Point in 1911 wearing a cocky cap, straggling tie, and oversized tweed jacket.

His 1915 West Point class picture shows him standing seriously straight in the front row (his right hand jammed Bonaparte-like into the front of his dress gray tunic), down the row from an equally dour Omar Bradley, his classmate. This is the same Cadet Eisenhower who controlled his temper by playing the goofy country bumpkin in front of upperclass martinets. After one corporal convicted Ike and another cadet of an infraction, they were ordered to report in "full dress coats" for punishment in the corporal's room. Eisenhower wrote in 1969, "At the appointed time, each of us donned full dress coats and with no other stitch of clothing, marched into the corporal's room." Both conspirators received added punishments.

There is also the face of a happy and proud young lieutenant standing with his new bride Mamie in 1916. As a lieutenant colonel he smiles broadly in his formal white dinner jacket once again with Douglas MacArthur, in Manila, 1935. He maintains impassive control at the revolting sight of the interior of a Nazi concentration camp in 1945. His joy at being home after the war is expressed in his exuberantly raised "V for Victory" hands as well as his broadly grinning face in a victory parade in New York City in June 1945. He shows obvious surprise at the news of President Truman's firing MacArthur in April 1951. Smiling modestly, he poses with Senator Robert Taft after beating the Ohioan for the 1952 Republican presidential nomination.

The one thing Ike's face always mirrored was genuineness, not the plasticity of a practiced politician. He was truly, for all his greatness, a man of the people. He was one of America's most loved twentieth-century men as well as one of the greatest presidents of his century. But let us see him as he was as we journey through Ike's life.

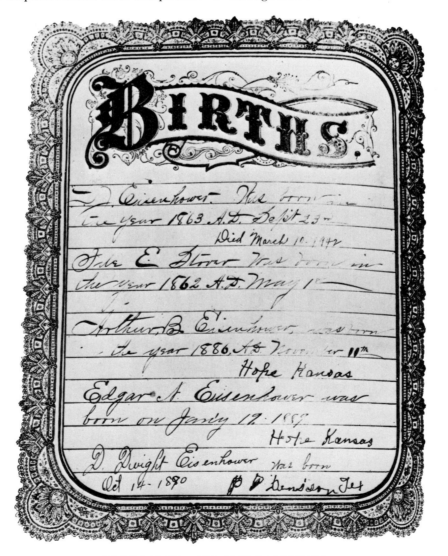

The family bible with birth entries for the three oldest Eisenhower boys. Note Ike's birth date at the bottom, October 14, 1890, in Denison, Texas, where they lived briefly while their father worked for the railroad.

CHAPTER 2

Abilene and West Point

"**I** come from the very heart of America," he said in his famous Guildhall address in London, June 12, 1945, celebrating the Allied victory over Germany. This heart of America was Abilene, Kansas, where he grew up and from where he left for West Point on a June day in 1911.

Dwight David Eisenhower was the third of six sons born to David and Ida Eisenhower. In 1878 fourteen-year-old David, Ike's father, had left the Susquehanna Valley of Pennsylvania with around three hundred members of a Mennonite group called the River Brethren. They headed west for the great plains of Kansas, where most became successful farmers. In time David attended Lane University, a small institution in Lecompton, Kansas, and met Ida Stover. She had migrated westward from the Shenandoah Valley of Virginia and, like David Eisenhower, had German Mennonite forebears. The two were married in September 1885, and David opened a general store in the small town of Hope, near Abilene.

But "drought and an invasion of grasshoppers" caused the Eisenhowers to go bankrupt a few years later. So David, Ida, and their two small sons moved to Denison, Texas, where David worked for the railroad. There a third son, Dwight—known a few years later as Ike—was born on October 14, 1890. About that time the River Brethren back in Abilene opened a new creamery and offered a mechanic's job to David. His acceptance meant that the family could return permanently to Kansas. Thus, in the spring of 1891, the Eisenhowers and baby Dwight moved to Abilene where his three younger brothers were born and the boys grew up.

In that part of Kansas the countryside has not changed much since Ike was a boy. A driver on Interstate 70 bound west for Denver or east for St. Louis sees gentle, rolling farmland much as it was early in the century. A little before Ike's time, however, Abilene had been a rough cow town, a meeting place for Texas cattlemen and the railroads east. For a time in 1871, the legendary Wild Bill Hickok had been marshal. During Ike's youth the town's population was around four thousand and Abilene was a typical small town of rural America at the turn of the century: there was no water system until 1902, and until 1910 the streets were unpaved.

David and Ida brought up Dwight and his brothers in an atmosphere of religion, discipline, and love. They assigned chores to the boys, and woe to the sleepyhead who missed the 5:00 A.M. starting time. Though poor, the family lived comfortably, raising most of its own food. To bring in some cash, the boys worked at odd jobs; Dwight earned money with his vegetable garden.

Although the Eisenhowers lived on the "wrong side of the tracks," Abilene was an egalitarian town, with all the children coming together in the schools. Dwight was an average student and well-liked, though his teachers considered him a roughneck. Fistfights were part of growing up in Wild Bill's town.

Besides their work, school, and Bible study, the well-organized Eisenhower brothers found time for play. Dwight liked baseball, football, boxing, skating, and above all, camping and hunting with his dog Flip. During these outdoor forays he became proficient in cooking over a campfire, which became a hobby in later life.

In late May 1909 Ike and his older brother Edgar both graduated from high school. Both wanted to continue their education, and Ed had decided on the University of Michigan to become a lawyer. But how could he afford it? Dwight came up with the solution: he would work for a year at the creamery to help support Ed, then the following year Ed would work so that Ike could go to school. Ed agreed and went to Michigan that September while Ike went to work. Though the year seemed to be a lost period of marking time, it gave Ike a chance to mature and presented him with an unexpected and golden opportunity.

In the summer of 1910 Ike became friends with Swede Hazlett, a local boy who had failed the entrance exam for the Naval Academy in Annapolis, Maryland, and was preparing for another try. He interested young Dwight in trying for it too, and they spent the summer studying together, thus giving Dwight the idea of applying for admission to the Naval Academy himself. What better way was there for a poor boy to get a college education? His letter to Senator Bristow brought the reply that, yes, in October Dwight could take the competitive examinations for the Naval Academy, and, oh yes, a place called West Point also had a vacancy if he wished to take its exam. As it turned out, Ike's October birthday meant that, at twenty, he was too old to become a midshipman. So it was fortunate that he took and passed the West Point exam and won an appointment to the United States Military Academy in New York.

In June 1911 the future supreme commander and president began the long rail journey from Kansas through Missouri to New York. He arrived at West Point's small station as one of 264 new cadets from all parts of the United States on June 14, 1911. That evening, they stood together on the plain of West Point to take the oath of office, a moment Ike never forgot. As he later wrote:

> A feeling came over me that the expression "the United States of America" would now and henceforth mean something different than it ever had before. From here on it would be the nation I would be serving, not myself.

Now came the training for new cadets in what was known as Beast Barracks, the air resounding with cries of "Shoulders back!" "Suck up that gut!" "Chin in, Mr. Dumbjohn!" Each cadet may have been the best athlete, scholar, or all-around boy in his part of the world, but the system was designed to socialize him as a West Point plebe, a member of the Army on the bottom rung. Some cadets could take it; some could not. Ike, although far from being a model cadet, took it in stride. After all, he was older and more mature than most of his classmates, and he badly wanted a college education.

West Point in the 1920s put cadets through a stern four-year regime based on tradition. Here was where cadet Ulysses S. Grant lived and where cadet George Custer learned to ride. The academy had not, in fact, changed much since their times. Regulations covered every detail of living, and the studies themselves were narrow and technical. While Ike was above the class average in academics, he also had a high number of demerits. The frontier spirit did not entirely leave him while he was at the Military Academy.

In sports, especially football, Ike found his outlet. In his second year he was a star—a very promising back, the New York papers said. Then disaster hit when he injured his knee during the 1912 game with Tufts. There could be no more football for Ike. He did coach the junior varsity team, and as a cheerleader he rallied the Cadet Corps on evenings before the games.

In June 1915 his graduating class numbered 164. World War II would make this the most famous of any West Point class, "the class the stars fell on." Fifty-nine were to become general officers; two of them, Ike and Omar Bradley, were to achieve the rarefied rank, general of the Army. But that was a long time off.

At West Point Ike absorbed much that would sustain him later: teamwork, obedience, acceptance of orders, and most importantly, the principle of duty first. (In these matters the Point reinforced Ida Eisenhower's standards.) He also accepted the notion of the time that his profession, the Regular Army, was distinct from those involved in making money. The Army was more of a priesthood and—ironically, in terms of what happened to Ike—a profession set aside from politics. By its very nature it was a profession that had a conservative, to the point of being hidebound, outlook.

Ida Stover, Ike's mother, as a young woman. Born in 1862 in the Shenandoah Valley of Virginia, she moved to Kansas in 1883 where she enrolled in Lane University and met fellow student, David Eisenhower.

Ida and David's wedding portrait. The ceremony took place in the Lane University chapel on September 23, 1885, David's twenty-second birthday.

David Eisenhower, Ike's father. A year younger than Ida, David had moved with his family and a large group of River Brethren from the Gettysburg, Pennsylvania, area to Kansas in 1879.

First-known photo of Dwight Eisenhower (1893). On the left is his oldest brother Arthur holding the baby Roy. Dwight stands in front of Edgar on the right.

The Smoky Hill River where Ike fished and played as a young boy.

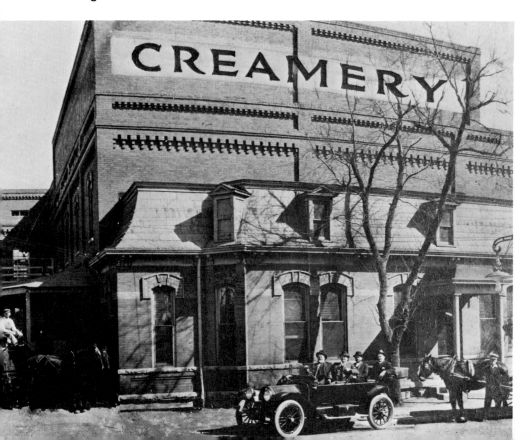

The creamery in Abilene where David was employed. Ike also worked there after high school and before he entered West Point.

Ike's boyhood home in Abilene, Kansas, where he lived from 1891 until he left for West Point in 1911.

Ike (second from left on the front row) and his fourth-grade class at Lincoln School in 1899. The Eisenhowers' tight budget meant that, unlike the other boys in his class, Ike had to wear overalls.

Ike in his seventh grade photo (1902), picking his teeth while his classmates pose solemnly for the record. His deportment grades were his lowest.

A page from the Abilene High School yearbook (1909). Ike and his brother Ed graduated the same year though Ed was two years older than Ike. Wanting to make money, he had dropped out of school for a while. Probably the brother closest to Ike, he went on to become a successful lawyer in Tacoma, Washington.

EDGAR NEWTON
EISENHOWER

♣

"Big Ike" is the greatest football player of the class. Also on his head there is a depression due to non-development of the conscious and over-development of the subconscious brain. Football teams '07, '08, '09. Base ball teams '07, '08, '09; captain '08.

DAVID DWIGHT
EISENHOWER

♣

"Little Ike," now a couple inches taller than "big Ike," is our best historian and mathematician. President of Athletic Association, '09; Football, '07, '08; Baseball '08, '09.

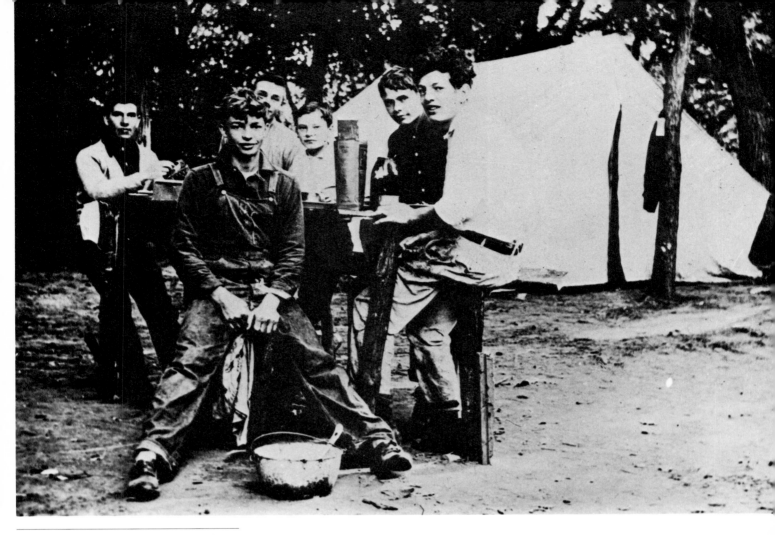

One of Ike's favorite boyhood pastimes was camping. He is shown in front here with some of his friends (1904).

Ike and his family (1902). *Front row, left to right:* David, Milton, and Ida; *back, left to right:* Ike, Edgar, Earl, Arthur, and Roy.

The Abilene High School baseball team, about 1908. Ike is second from right, top row.

A family photo taken in 1910, when Ike worked in the creamery before going to West Point. *From left*: Milton, David, Ike, Ida, and Earl. In front of Ida is Ike's dog, Flip, who had run away from a passing circus to become an Eisenhower.

Ike's letter (on facing page) to Senator Bristow concerning his appointment to West Point. Note that Ike dropped a year from his age, a remarkable error for Abilene High School's best mathematician.

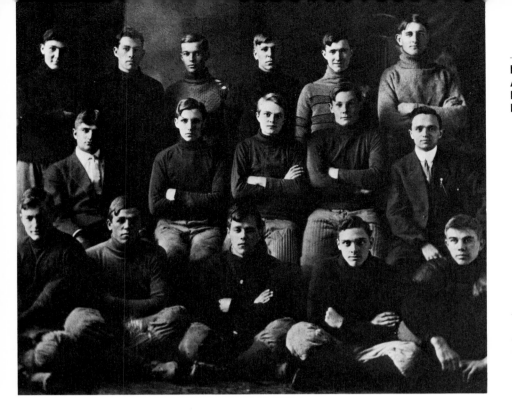

Ike (third from left, top row) and the Abilene High School football team. To his right is "Six" McDonald, one of his close friends.

Ike, in what appears to be a hand-me-down jacket, on a stopover in Chicago en route from Abilene to West Point. He entered the academy as one of 265 plebes on June 14; four years later 164 of them graduated.

Abilene, Kansas.
Oct. 25, 1910.

Sen. J. L. Bristow,
Salina, Kans.

Dear Sir:

You letter of the 24th instant has just been received. I wish to thank you sincerely for the favor you have shown me in appointing me to West Point.

In regard to the information desired; I am just nineteen years and eleven days of age, and have been a resident of Abilene, Kans. for eighteen years.

Thanking you again, I am

very truly yours,

Dwight Eisenhower

A dignified and serious Ike in a formal cadet photograph. He appears to have come a long way from the boy picking his teeth in the seventh grade photo—at least outwardly. He was 125th out of 164 in his class in demerits.

During his first-class year, Ike was a color sergeant. Third from left, he is holding the Corp of Cadet's flag. The photo was taken in old Camp Clinton, a summer encampment across the plain from the academy buildings.

The 1912 Army football team (bottom). Ike (second from left) played left halfback. The next-to-last player on the right is Omar Bradley, a cadet from Missouri. They are, respectively (photo on left), third from left in the middle row and third from right, top row.

At this point, early in the 1912 season, Ike was one of West Point's outstanding football players. Later in the fall a knee injury in the Tufts game cost him his football career.

Ike's graduation photograph (1915) as a member of the class "the stars fell on." Out of its 164 members, 59 became generals. Its nearest competitor was the class of 1917, which produced 43 generals.

3

Brown Shoe Army

When Second Lieutenant Dwight Eisenhower graduated from West Point in June 1915, World War I forces had been slaughtering Europeans for almost a year. The isolationist United States, however, was still very much at peace; American participation in the war was not to come for another two years. Ike entered a peacetime Army.

His first post was with the Nineteenth Infantry at Fort Sam Houston in San Antonio, Texas. There he met an attractive, vivacious girl of eighteen, Mamie Geneva Doud, daughter of a wealthy Denver family that wintered in San Antonio. On Valentine's Day 1916 they were engaged; five months later on July 1, 1916, they were married. Coincidently, Ike became a first lieutenant on his wedding day.

After America declared war on Germany in 1917, Eisenhower tried unsuccessfully to get himself assigned overseas. Instead he was sent to Gettysburg, Pennsylvania, to command a camp for training in new and untested weapons—tanks. Ike was so good at this job, which included dealing with visitors from Congress, that some years later he received the Distinguished Service Medal for it. But his expertise also kept him there for the rest of the war. Although it was good experience, it was not combat, and this bothered Ike for the next quarter-century.

After "the war to end all wars" was over, one routine assignment followed another. Ike became so discouraged that he considered quitting the Army. And it was during this time that tragedy entered his life. In January 1921 Mamie and Dwight's three-year-old son and only child Doud Dwight, called Icky, died of scarlet fever. As Ike wrote nearly a half-century later:

> This was the greatest disappointment and disaster of my life, the one I have never been able to forget completely. Today when I think of it, even now as I write of it, the keenness of our loss comes back to me as fresh and terrible as it was in that long dark day. . . .

One of Ike's routine assignments was to prove invaluable because it was at Camp Meade, Maryland, he got to know George Patton who had seen combat in France. Ike shared Patton's enthusiasm for the tank's potential as a new offensive weapon. (In fact, Ike's advanced views on the subject as set forth in an article brought a warning from the chief of infantry to stop publishing anything incompatible with infantry thinking.) And it was through Patton that Eisenhower met General Fox Conner, an 1898 West Point graduate who had been General John J. Pershing's operations officer in France.

Conner was the first of three generals Eisenhower served who greatly influenced Ike's thoughts and life. Ike so impressed Conner that, when the general was sent to a command in Panama in the early 1920s, he managed to have Ike assigned to him as executive officer. Ike was promoted to major, a promotion that came only one month after his demotion to captain.

Conner had the reputation of being one of the smartest officers in the Army. He was particularly interested in military history, especially its philosophers and great captains such as Napoleon. When Eisenhower worked for Conner, he was required to read serious military literature that the two of them then discussed, analyzing the reasons for decisions and their effect upon the outcome of the battles. In essence, this Panama assignment was a graduate education in military arts for Ike. It was a fulfilling time for Ike. And the summer of 1922 was happy in another way with the arrival of Mamie and Ike's second child, John Sheldon Doud Eisenhower.

Conner—not the infantry branch—arranged for Ike to become a student at the Army's prestigious Command and General Staff School at Fort Leavenworth, Kansas, in 1925. It was there that Eisenhower first stood out from his contemporaries.

Competing with 275 of the best officers in the Army, the indifferent student of West Point days graduated first in his class. This was an immense career step for Ike; he was now a young officer who was going places.

Still Eisenhower's patron, in 1927 Fox Conner had him assigned to an important job with the Battle Monuments Commission, which was headed by General Pershing. Ike's first duty, working in Pershing's Washington, D.C., office, was to write a guidebook to the World War I battlefields. Ike's work resulted in a strong letter of commendation from Pershing. A short time later, in 1927, Ike achieved the goal of every officer who hoped someday to be a general: selection for the Army War College in Washington, D.C.

When he graduated in 1928, he was sent to Europe to write a revised edition of the guidebook. Now he could actually visit the battlefields of the "Great War," traveling leisurely over what had reverted to farmlands and forests. In 1929, the year that would bring the Great Depression, Ike was assigned to Washington to the office of the assistant secretary of war, where he worked on industrial mobilization.

There he encountered the Army Chief of Staff Douglas MacArthur, who assumed that position November 21, 1930. MacArthur was the second of the generals who tremendously influenced Ike's life. Soon he had Eisenhower writing speeches and reports, and in time MacArthur made him an immediate assistant. The relationship was to last until the end of 1939.

When MacArthur's tour as Army chief of staff ended in 1935, he retired from active duty and went to Manila as military adviser to President Manuel Quezon of the new Philippine commonwealth government. To Ike's dismay, instead of getting a troop assignment, MacArthur insisted on taking him along to the Philippines. Becoming MacArthur's day-to-day contact with Quezon, Eisenhower soon made himself indispensable to the general.

What were the qualities Eisenhower had that made MacArthur depend on him? He was a brilliant worker who loyally supported his chief's decisions, he adjusted to MacArthur's time schedules and whims, and he learned to think from the general's point of view. These MacArthur years were also valuable to Ike. To what he had learned from Fox Conner, he could now add a broad perspective and see matters as a head of state would. Later on, he said that he was "deeply grateful for the administrative experience" he gained under MacArthur without which he "would not have been ready for the great responsibilities of the war."

While Eisenhower had tremendous respect for MacArthur, their temperaments were quite different. MacArthur's enormous ego contrasted with Ike's tolerance and forthrightness, so they could never be really close. As his Philippines tour drew to a close in 1939, Ike looked forward not only to a change of bosses but to getting back to troops.

When World War II broke out in Europe in September 1939, Lieutenant Colonel Eisenhower immediately requested a transfer to the United States. Ike hoped for a troop assignment in what surely would be a major buildup of forces since the war clouds were undoubtedly headed for America. He left the Philippines in December 1939 for troop duty at Fort Lewis, Washington, helping to train inductees for the new expanding army. When Germany swept through Norway, Denmark, the Low Countries, and France in swift succession during the spring of 1940, the U.S. government called for the first peacetime military draft. Ike soon became chief of staff of the Third Division and later of the Ninth Army Corps, an assignment that carried with it his temporary promotion to colonel in March 1941.

On the day of Ike's promotion, President Franklin D. Roosevelt signed into law the lend-lease bill, which in effect allied the United States with the British cause. In June 1941 the war reached an early peak with the German invasion of Russia; for the moment at least, Nazi forces seemed unstoppable. One thing was clear: the U.S. Army had better be ready for combat. No one knew this better than General George C. Marshall, who, as Army chief of staff, arranged the largest peacetime military maneuvers ever held in the United States. As well as training the troops, these maneuvers gave the top Army brass a chance to observe officers for selection into the small group of generals who later would command the American forces in World War II. Eisenhower was named chief of staff for Lieutenant General Walter Krueger, commander of the Third Army. Krueger's forces engaged those commanded by Lieutenant General Ben Lear during the exercises.

In September 1941, amid torrential winds and rain in Louisiana, Krueger's Third Army won the mock battles. Eisenhower's staff work received a great deal of credit, and for the first time his name (sometimes misspelled) appeared in press dispatches. Within a small sphere he had made his mark, and at the end of the maneuvers on September 29, Marshall promoted Eisenhower to the temporary rank of brigadier general. Twenty-six years after graduating from West Point, Ike was on his way.

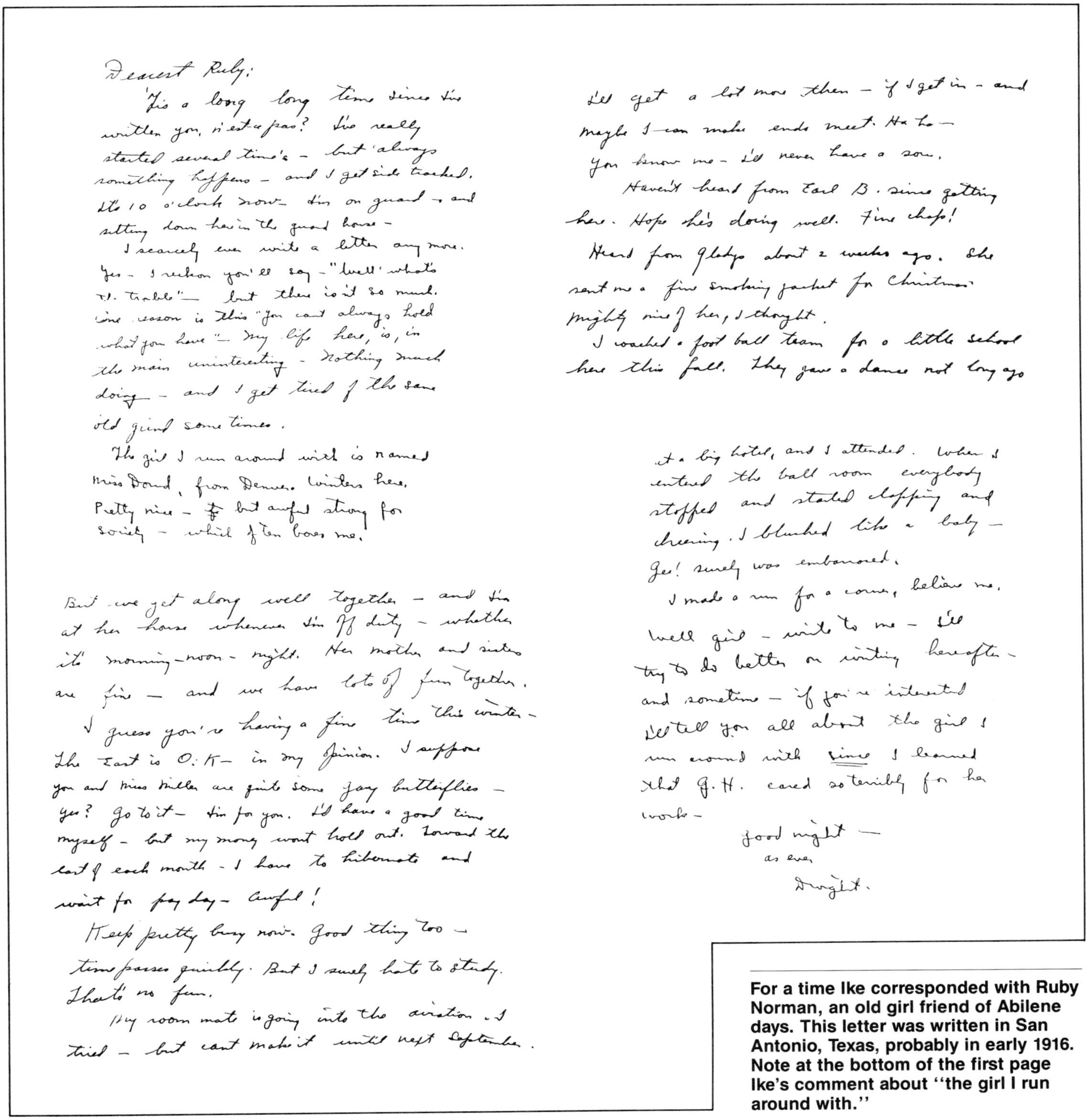

Dearest Ruby:

'Tis a long long time since tis written you, is'nt it pao? I've really started several time's - but always something happens - and I get side tracked. It's 10 o'clock now - tis on guard - and sitting down here in the guard house -

I scarcely ever write a letter any more. Yes - I reckon you'll say - "well what's the trouble" - but there is'nt so much. One reason is this "you can't always hold what you have" - my life here, is, in the main uninteresting - Nothing much doing - and I get tired of the same old grind some times.

The girl I run around with is named Miss Doud, from Denver. Winters here. Pretty nice - but awful strong for society - which often bores me.

But we get along well together - and tis at her house whenever I'm off duty - whether it's morning-noon-night. Her mother and sisters are fine - and we have lots of fun together.

I guess you're having a fine time this winter - the East is O.K. in my opinion. I suppose you and Miss Miller are quite some gay butterflies - yes? go to it - tis for you. I'd have a good time myself - but my money won't hold out. Toward the last of each month - I have to hibernate and wait for pay day - awful!

I keep pretty busy now. Good thing too - time passes quickly. But I surely hate to study. That's no fun.

My room mate is going into the aviation. I tried - but can't make it until next September.

I'll get a lot more then - if I get in - and maybe I can make ends meet. Ha ha - you know me - I'll never have a sou.

Haven't heard from Earl B. since getting here. Hope he's doing well. Fine chap!

Heard from Gladys about 2 weeks ago. She sent me a fine smoking jacket for Christmas - mighty nice of her, I thought.

I coached a foot ball team for a little school here this fall. They gave a dance not long ago at a big hotel, and I attended. When I entered the ball room everybody stopped and started clapping and cheering. I blushed like a baby - Gee! surely was embarrassed.

I made a run for a corner, believe me. Well girl - write to me - I'll try to do better on writing hereafter - and sometime - if you're interested I'll tell you all about the girl I run around with since I learned that G.H. cared so terribly for her work -

good night -

as ever,

Dwight.

For a time Ike corresponded with Ruby Norman, an old girl friend of Abilene days. This letter was written in San Antonio, Texas, probably in early 1916. Note at the bottom of the first page Ike's comment about "the girl I run around with."

Mamie Geneva Doud at the age of 15.
At his first post in Fort Sam Houston
(1915), Ike met eighteen-year-old
Mamie.

Ike and Mamie during their courting
days.

Ike and Mamie were married in the
Doud house at 750 Lafayette Street,
Denver. Here the bride and groom
pose for their wedding picture (July
1916).

After a brief wedding trip to Abilene so Mamie could meet her in-laws, the newlyweds settled down in a three-room apartment at Fort Sam Houston, Texas—Apartment B, Building 617, Old Infantry Post. It soon became known as ''Club Eisenhower'' due to the popularity of the young couple. Mamie once said, ''I've kept house in everything but an igloo,'' and indeed this was the first of 35 moves in the first 35 years of their marriage!

Ike while pulling duty near the Mexican border in the fall of 1916. The future supreme commander looks less than inspired watching the men digging trenches.

Ike spent a frustrating time during World War I since he did not get to see combat. Instead, he was assigned to Camp Meade, Maryland, and Camp Colt, Pennsylvania, where he trained men in the primitive tanks of that day.

Now a captain, Ike was regimental supply officer of the Fifty-seventh Infantry in Leon Springs, Texas (May 1917).

Lieutenant Colonel Dwight Eisenhower, Mamie, and their first child, Doud Dwight (Icky). Ike was commanding officer of the Tank Training Center, Camp Colt, Gettysburg, Pennsylvania, in the spring of 1918. Icky was born on September 24, 1917, and died of scarlet fever January 2, 1921. It was a loss from which Ike never recovered. As he wrote nearly fifty years later, "This was the greatest disappointment and disaster in my life, the one I have never been able to forget completely."

He also coached camp football teams. Here he is in his old West Point letter sweater at Camp Meade (1920).

They lived at 237 Spring Avenue in Gettysburg, Pennsylvania, when Ike commanded Camp Colt (1918).

In 1919, the Army decided to send a truck convoy from coast to coast to test its vehicles on the mostly unpaved roads of the United States of those days, to show Americans the kinds of equipment used during the war, and to dramatize the lack of main highways in the country. The convoy left Washington, D.C., July 7 and arrived in San Francisco, California, on September 6, averaging approximately five miles an hour on the trip. Ike jumped at the chance to join the expedition. As he said in his entertaining account of the two-month trip in *At Ease*, he wanted to go along "partly for a lark and partly to learn." He and a friend, Major Serano Brett, did find the jaunt great fun, hunting, fishing, and playing poker and practical jokes. But there was a serious side to the experience as well, for this was probably when Ike first got the idea for one of the great achievements during his presidency four decades later—the U.S. Interstate Highway System.

Brett & J.

The most important event during Ike's Panama tour was the birth of his and Mamie's second child, John Sheldon Doud. At the baby's christening at the Doud family home in Denver, September 1922, one can see the pride and delight of the young father as he tenderly gazes down at the month-old baby he holds in his arms.

Ike and John in Panama, where the family lived from 1922 to 1924.

John, age one (1923). Ike said he so resembled Icky in appearance he could not tell their baby pictures apart.

In the summer of 1926 Ike visited Abilene after graduating first in his class from the Command and General Staff School at Fort Leavenworth, Kansas. Here he poses with his parents and brothers on the front porch of his boyhood home. By now each son had his own profession. *From left:* Roy, a pharmacist; Arthur, a banker; Earl, an engineer; Edgar, a lawyer; and Milton, in the consular service. Ike was at this point a 36-year-old major.

They lived at Camp Lorillard. Mamie described their house as "a double-decked shanty, only twice as disreputable."

General Fox Conner, known as one of the Army's "brains" and one of the three most important generals who influenced Ike's career. As Ike's boss in Panama from 1922–24, he insisted on the young officer's studying military arts and the great captains. At the end of his life, Ike would remember Conner as "the ablest man I ever knew."

At Leavenworth, they lived in Apartment 2C, Otis Hall.

The Wyoming apartment building in Washington, D.C., the Eisenhowers' home from 1927 to 1928 and from 1930 to 1935.

In Paris they were at 68 quai d'Auteil (1928–29).

Mamie, looking very Parisian (1929).

Ike and Mamie on a visit to San Remo, Italy, during that period.

In 1929 Ike returned to Washington to work in the office of the assistant secretary of war. Subsequently he became Army Chief of Staff Douglas MacArthur's aide in the early 1930s. This famous picture shows MacArthur mopping his face—and Ike smoking in the background—when facing the Bonus Marchers in 1932. Against Ike's advice, MacArthur personally led the troops that evicted the Bonus Marchers from a temporary encampment they had set up near the Capitol building.

In 1935 MacArthur retired and became military adviser to President Manuel Quezon of the new Philippine government. To Ike's chagrin MacArthur insisted on his coming, too. Here he stands behind MacArthur as both salute with their boaters at the arrival ceremony (October 23, 1935).

MacArthur with aides Eisenhower and T.J. Davis at the Malacanang Palace (1935).

While in the Philippines Ike shaved his head for comfort. His job was more than just an aide's: he became the liaison between the American proconsul and the Philippine president. Ike began to acquire a flair for diplomacy on this job.

Ike, Mamie, and son John, just turned 15, in Manila (August 4, 1937), where they lived in the air-conditioned Manila Hotel.

Ike had enjoyed outdoor activities since boyhood when camping, hunting, and fishing were favorite pastimes. Physically active, sports had always been important to him, with football his favorite game. As an adult he took up golf and became unusually proficient at the sport, achieving a respectable handicap. He had the ability to utterly concentrate on whatever he was doing, so that these activities wonderfully liberated him from professional burdens of the moment. Here he is after a golf game in the Philippines, 1937.

On leave during a trip home to the United States (July 1938), Ike and Mamie pose with the captain of the S.S. *President Coolidge*, K.A. Ahlin, who inscribed the picture "to my very dear friends and shipmates."

Ike spent some of his leave in Abilene with his parents. His son John took this picture of Ike with Ida.

In late 1939, with war under way in Europe, Ike requested a transfer to the United States. At his final ceremony in the Philippines, President Quezon, a great admirer of Ike, looks on as Mamie pins the Philippine government's Distinguished Service Cross on Ike (December 12, 1939).

When he returned to the States, Eisenhower joined the Fifteenth Infantry Regiment in early 1940 and ended up at Fort Lewis, Washington. He then became chief of staff of the Third Division, the regiment's parent headquarters. In March 1941 he was promoted to full colonel and made chief of staff of the Ninth Army Corps, still at Fort Lewis. Here he is toward the end of his tour. Incidentally, in spite of the high rank he achieved, the promotion to ''bird'' colonel meant more to Ike than any other.

The Eisenhower quarters at Fort Lewis, Washington.

(August 1941) Ike, now chief of staff, Third Army, Fort Sam Houston, Texas, with his boss Lieutenant General Walter Krueger as they arrive at Lake Charles, Louisiana, to begin the great Louisiana maneuvers against Lieutenant General Ben ''Yoo Hoo'' Lear's Second Army. With them is Lieutenant Colonel Oliver H. Stout, c.o. of the 113 Observation Squadron. The mock battle took place in two phases in late September.

Ike working with Lieutenant General Lesley J. McNair, maneuver director (mid-September 1941). Krueger's ''blues'' subsequently won the maneuver against Lear's ''reds,'' and Eisenhower's staff work was given much of the credit. For the first time, he was mentioned in press releases. At the end of the maneuvers, George Marshall, Army chief of staff, promoted him to brigadier general. Ike had arrived.

Ike as chief of staff with the Ninth Army Corps conferring with Lieutenant Colonel Jim Bradley at a military exercise in California (June 1941).

CHAPTER 4

General Ike

Ike shortly after his promotion to brigadier general (fall 1941). This photo was used by the wire services and was part of the initial publicity accorded Ike in connection with the Louisiana maneuvers.

On December 7, 1941, less than three months after Ike's promotion to brigadier general, came the Japanese attack on Pearl Harbor. Within days the United States was at war with both Japan and the Axis powers of Germany and Italy. Chief of Staff George Marshall needed a planning officer who knew both the Far East and its American commander MacArthur, now back on active duty. Dwight D. Eisenhower met those qualifications perfectly, and at Marshall's summons he left his station at Fort Sam Houston, Texas, for duty in Washington, D.C. George Marshall became the third—and the most important—general in Eisenhower's career.

Ike arrived in Washington on December 14, 1941. No one knew it at the time, but he was about to begin training to be the supreme commander.

Though Marshall seemed cold and austere, he was not difficult to work with, and Ike quickly became his protégé. Newly promoted Major General Eisenhower was placed in charge of war planning, which by the summer of 1942 was more concerned with Europe than with the Far East. Ike's ability to get along with the other agencies, including the Navy, was impressive, and on a trip to England, he was a great hit with the British.

The immediate problem in England was how to build up American forces and supplies for later use in military operations; furthermore, someone was needed there to take over as American commander. In June 1942 Marshall picked Eisenhower as the commander of the European Theater of Operations, with President Roosevelt's enthusiastic backing. At the time it seemed like a temporary arrangement; the feeling was that Marshall himself would head any American military operations on the European continent.

The day after he arrived in England, Ike held a press conference, for now the world was watching him. This conference was the first of some five hundred he was to hold over the next twenty years. No other public figure of the time, except Franklin Delano Roosevelt, had such close scrutiny from or was so popular with the press and was so skillful in dealing with it.

British and American strategists had to decide on basic operational questions. Should the strategy, as the Americans favored, be that of direct approach—an invasion across the English Channel in 1943? Or as the British believed, would an indirect approach—clearing the Mediterranean first—have better results? With Roosevelt's support, the British prevailed: Operation Torch, the invasion of North Africa to sweep out the German forces, became the objective. The command of the Allied invasion went to Eisenhower. In a matter of months he had gone from being an American commander to an Allied commander and was promoted to the rank of lieutenant general.

On November 5, 1942, Ike moved his headquarters to Gibraltar. Three days later some 300,000 British, American, and Free French troops under his command invaded French North Africa. The targets were Casablanca on the Atlantic and Oran and Algiers on the Mediterranean.

To minimize French resistance from the Vichy government set up after Hitler conquered France, the Allies had spirited General Henri Giraud, a German prisoner, out of France to work with Eisenhower in commanding French forces in North Africa. The local French commanders, however, ignored Giraud. When the Allies captured Admiral Jean Darlan, overall commander of Vichy military forces, Ike enlisted his help, feeling that the French forces would listen to Darlan. This decision caused a furor, especially arousing columnists and commentators. This early experience with the "Darlan deal" was Eisenhower's initiation into handling political problems as a commander and caused him to make, as he later put it, "the first major political decision I had ever felt called on to make."

The invasion of French North Africa, despite resistance by the French at Oran and Casablanca, was successful. All the area west of Algiers was in Allied hands three days after the landing. Meanwhile, in an action timed to support the landing, Commander of the British Eighth Army General Bernard Montgomery broke out of El Alamein west of Alexandria, Egypt, on October 25 and began driving German General Erwin Rommel and his Afrika Korps before him. With Montgomery advancing westward and Eisenhower pushing eastward toward Tunisia, the Allies were squeezing German and Italian forces into a pocket.

It was a difficult campaign, lasting from the fall of 1942 to the spring of 1943. As the fighting climaxed, Eisenhower's American forces held a line on the west while Montgomery's forces, now also under Eisenhower's command, faced the enemy from the south and east. Eventually, linking the two forces sealed the fate of the Axis forces in Africa. In the last week alone of the campaign, the Allies captured 240,000 prisoners. The first and probably most trying of all of Ike's campaigns was over on May 13.

During the North African fighting, American forces and commanders, including Eisenhower, were still learning, and they gave a mixed performance. Added to Ike's concerns—besides the political mix-up with the French—were coordination problems between the various services as well as with the British, since each nation's military force had its own way of doing things.

Meanwhile, in January 1943, Roosevelt and British Prime Minister Winston Churchill held a summit conference in Casablanca. They decided to continue Mediterranean operations that year, first in Sicily and then on the Italian mainland. The goal was to knock Italy out of the war. This decision to concentrate on the Mediterranean postponed cross-Channel operations until 1944. In 1943, Ike became a four-star general. The lieutenant colonel of three years before had quickly climbed to the top of the ladder.

On July 10, 1943, southeastern Sicily saw the greatest amphibious-force landing up to that time. The British Eighth Army under Montgomery and the U.S. Seventh Army under George Patton—both commanded by Eisenhower—set foot on a number of beaches. In less than six weeks, the entire island was in the hands of the Allies. Thus they captured a strategic location, a stage for invading Italy. In the course of the Sicilian fighting, the Allies captured around 14,000 Axis troops, primarily Italian; an additional 30,000 were killed. Allied casualties were around 25,000.

During the Sicilian campaign, the Italians deposed their dictator Mussolini, who was Hitler's crony, and a new government under Marshal Pietro Badoglio took over. Negotiations now began to get Italy out of the war, but they were complicated by increasing German troops in Italy. Although the Italians were eager to surrender, they wanted to protect themselves from the Nazis. Finally, on September 8, 1943, Eisenhower and Badoglio broadcast announcements of Italy's capitulation to the Allies.

Meanwhile, Ike planned and prepared for the invasion of mainland Italy, still held by the Germans. On September 3, against little resistance, Montgomery put portions of the British Eighth Army into the toe of the Italian boot. On September 9 the equivalent of four divisions of an American army commanded by General Mark Clark began going ashore at Salerno just south of Naples. This was a treacherous operation; the enemy expected it and responded with massive counterattacks that made the beachhead extremely dangerous. The Germans threatened at times to wipe out the American force. But the Americans overcame the threat, held and expanded the beachhead, and came ashore with reinforcements and supplies. The Italian campaign itself, though, was to drag on for another twenty months before complete occupation toward the end of the European war.

What about Ike's performance as an Allied commander in the Mediterranean? Remember that he had been a staff officer for over twenty years; this was his first combat experience. Initially, he was unsure of himself, making some early mistakes against the Germans in North Africa. He then became a confident but cautious commander. His operations in Sicily and Italy also reflect this attitude. Fortunately, through these operations as well as during the earlier political problems with the French, he always had the support of the American Chief of Staff Marshall.

Eisenhower's great contribution in the Mediterranean was his insistence that the British and American services work together as true allies. His emphasis on teamwork perhaps led to his preeminence. In December 1943 Roosevelt told Ike that Marshall would stay in Washington and gave Ike command of the joint cross-Channel operation scheduled for 1944. It was given the code name of Overlord. Without the Overlord command, Eisenhower would have been just another World War II general; with Overlord he became one of the most famous Americans of the twentieth century.

The Japanese destroying the American Pacific Fleet in Pearl Harbor, Sunday morning, December 7, 1941. Everyone later remembered the moment they heard about the news on that fateful day. Brigadier General Dwight Eisenhower was at his quarters in Fort Sam Houston taking a nap when the word came. For Eisenhower, the day that would "live in infamy" marked the start of a series of events bringing him from obscurity to world fame.

Summoned to Washington shortly after Pearl Harbor by Army Chief of Staff George Marshall, Ike was placed in charge of War Plans where he was promoted to major general. Marshall then selected him to command the American forces in Europe. Shown here is Ike's first press conference after assuming the new command in London (June 1942). The following month Ike was promoted to lieutenant general.

Soon after arriving in London, General Eisenhower met French General Charles de Gaulle, a symbol of French resistance to the Nazis since May 1940. The naval officer on Ike's right is U.S. Naval Commander in Europe Admiral Harold Stark.

In London in late September 1942 with his Chief of Staff Brigadier General Walter Bedell Smith, who remained with Ike the entire war, and Major General Mark Clark, his deputy.

Ike at his desk just after he had issued orders for the invasion of French Morocco (October 1942).

On November 5, 1942, Ike moved his headquarters to Gibralter and directed the invasion of French North Africa with over 300,000 British, U.S., and Free French troops. The troops easily captured Algiers but encountered French resistance at Oran and further west at Casablanca. Ike is seen here with General Mark Clark laying it on the line to Admiral Jean Darlan, the captured Vichy leader whom Ike felt was the key to French cooperation in North Africa.

Ike's notes at the peak of his frustrations (January 1943). The green American troops had been repulsed in December in their attempt to capture Tunis and Bizerte, the supply-line ports vital to German and Italian forces in North Africa. Meanwhile Bernard Montgomery's Eighth Army was pushing westward as part of an Anglo-American effort to capture all of Tunisia and destroy Rommel's Afrika Korps.

January 19, 1943

Written by Ike about January 19th and stuck in his desk — said it was to "clarify" his thoughts

Ike at his headquarters in the St. Georges Hotel in the center of Algiers (early 1943). He was promoted to four-star rank in February; only two years before he had been a lieutenant colonel.

Ike with Kay Summersby, his driver and aide in Algiers (early 1943). She later wrote a sensational book indicating their relationship became a romantic one, but the allegations have never been substantiated.

Ike in his office at the St. Georges reading a letter from Mamie (early 1943).

On May 16, 1943, Ike pinned a third star on his old friend George Patton. They had been pioneers together in armored tactics back in the twenties at Camp Meade.

Ike always enjoyed being with "his" men and visited the troops in North Africa (1943).

Tunis fell May 13, 1943. Demoralized and completely encircled, the Axis troops surrendered in great numbers; over 240,000 were taken as prisoners. Ike and French General Henri Giraud inspect French troops in Tunis on May 20. The two generals salute prior to Giraud presenting Eisenhower with the Grand Cross of the Legion of Honor on May 29.

Ike held an informal press conference with General Marshall at Allied Headquarters in North Africa on May 27, 1943, and announced "all the enemy in Tunisia is now either killed or captured."

Winston Churchill meeting with Allied leaders in his Algiers headquarters at the end of the Tunisian campaign (April 4, 1943). Planning was under way for the continuation of the Mediterranean campaign. *From left to right around Churchill:* Anthony Eden, Sir Alan Brooke, Air Chief Marshal Arthur Tedder, Admiral Sir Andrew Cunningham, and Generals Alexander, Marshall, Eisenhower, and Montgomery.

The Allied invasion of Sicily followed the Tunisian campaign by about two months, beginning July 10, 1943. One of its purposes was to intensify the pressure on Italy, the first of the three Axis countries scheduled for invasion, to surrender. Here Ike is greeted at the Palermo airport by General Patton.

American troops advancing from Caltanissetta toward Palermo in northern Sicily. By August 17 the occupation of Sicily was complete, though a well-executed withdrawal enabled the Germans to save the bulk of their forces.

The Allies launched their invasion of Italy on September 3, 1943. The main thrust was the Salerno landing, led by the Fifth American Army under Lieutenant General Mark Clark, on September 9. Fighting was fierce, but by October 8 the beachhead was secure. Ike, the overall commander, and Clark leave the Third Division war room (October 22) as the fighting up the peninsula continues at the Volturno River line.

General Eisenhower with Major General John A. Crane, Thirteenth Field Artillery Brigade commander, after visiting the Fifth Army front (December 19, 1943).

From the President to Marshal Stalin

The immediate appointment of General Eisenhower to command of Overlord operation has been decided upon.

Roosevelt

Cairo, Dec. 7. 43

Dear Eisenhower, I thought you might like to have this as a memento. It was written very hurriedly by me as the final meeting broke up yesterday, the President signing it immediately.
G.C.M.

In Cairo on the night of December 6, 1943, President Franklin Roosevelt dictated this message to Marshall and then signed it. Ike found out about his appointment the following day directly from Roosevelt. Sitting with Ike in a limousine in Tunis, Roosevelt turned to him and said, "Well, Ike, you are going to command Overlord."

Two days after his appointment to command the cross-Channel invasion, Eisenhower conferred with the president aboard *The Sacred Cow* en route to Sicily (December 8, 1943).

(December 27, 1943) Ike meets the press at Allied Headquarters in Algiers after his appointment as Overlord commander was announced.

Ike and FDR visit an airfield in Sicily.

A shot of Mamie in Washington, D.C.
(Christmas time, 1943). She had just
found out Ike was to be the supreme
commander for the Allied invasion of
Europe.

Supreme Commander

Ike watches the landing operation from
the deck of the British warship *Apollo*,
somewhere in the English Channel
(June 7, 1944).

By early 1944 Eisenhower was ready to take up his new duties as supreme commander. No American had ever held or would be likely to hold again a military command of this magnitude. The land forces alone comprised three Army groups, nine armies, 23 corps, and 87 divisions. Just outside London Ike established Supreme Headquarters Allied Expeditionary Forces (SHAEF). It was a headquarters absolutely without precedent, a true international staff in which national differences were submerged as much as possible.

Eisenhower's task was to bring together and prepare the forces of the many and diverse nations in the Allied command for the assault on Hitler's Europe. This was an invasion the world was waiting for and one the Soviets had long demanded to relieve the unremitting pressure of the German forces that had been fighting in Russia since June 1941. From January to the spring of 1944 men and materials poured into Great Britain until it seemed as if that grand island would sink. Training and planning for the complex assault proceeded apace.

The invasion was scheduled for June 5, 1944, but the weather was horrendous with winds rising to forty miles an hour. Ike was in a quandary. The troops were ready and waiting, most already loaded in vessels, and their fine edge could not last. When it finally appeared that there might be a break in the weather on the sixth, Ike gambled. "Well, we'll go," he decided, and the mighty armada of over one million men began the "Great Crusade."

June 6, 1944, a date for the history books, is also one of those days that, like Pearl Harbor, will always remain in the minds of people who heard the news that day. Ever after, they knew where they were and what they were doing when the word *D-Day* flashed around the world. The assault was led by the American First Army on Utah and Omaha beaches and by the British Second Army on Gold, Juno, and Sword beaches.

The Allies surprised the Germans, whose troops were concentrated at Calais and who considered Normandy relatively unimportant. Because the Nazis at first did not recognize the landing as the Allied main effort, Hitler withheld his reserves until too late. But mainly the magnificent heroism of the Allied forces made D-Day successful. Even Soviet dictator Stalin was impressed. "One must admit," he said, "that military history does not know a similar enterprise so broadly conceived on so huge a scale so masterfully executed."

By the end of the first week, with over 325,000 of their troops in France, the Allies had established a continuous sixty-mile-wide beachhead. On July 25 the Allies broke out of Normandy and, in accordance with Eisenhower's concept, fanned out in a broad front. At this point George Patton and his tank-heavy Third Army were unleashed for the great race across France. Falling back toward the Seine, the Germans suffered enormous losses in troops and weapons of war.

A problem soon arose for Eisenhower: what should he do about liberating Paris? In the City of Light the French were rising against their occupiers of the past four years. Feeling it was appropriate to have a French division be the liberators of the capital, Ike moved one to the fore with the Americans not far behind. Officially, the city was liberated on August 25, and the free world celebrated.

Meanwhile, the Allied armies moved across France, chasing a disorganized foe who avoided any major engagement. What made this extremely rapid pursuit possible was Ike's earlier insistence on the logistics to supply large mobile forces. In the middle of the race across France, General Alexander Patch's U.S. Seventh Army landed in southern France against comparatively light opposition and soon took its position on Patton's south flank.

At the end of the first ninety days, Eisenhower had achieved some remarkable results: the Atlantic wall had been breached, over 300,000 prisoners had been captured, and most of France and Belgium had been liberated. But now, despite extraordinary efforts, supplies could no longer keep up with the dramatic Allied advance. By September Ike found himself up against the German "West Wall" in operations designed to engage the enemy along a broad front, trying to get the Germans to commit their reserves in defensive battles. But Hitler had other plans.

Because Eisenhower concentrated his forces in areas where his offensive actions would bring the greatest results, some Allied-controlled areas were lightly held. Only four American divisions, two of them without battle experience, for example, held an eighty-mile defense line across the Ardennes Forest on the Belgium-German border. Hitler had been secretly concentrating his forces, under the code name Autumn Smoke, for a massive attack in that area. On December 16, 1944, the Germans struck. Just the day before, Ike had received his fifth star for a newly created rank; he was now General of the Army Eisenhower.

The Germans launched their counteroffensive early in the morning during foul weather. Their goal was to seize the vital port of Antwerp and to destroy Allied armies in the north. Under its most able commander Field Marshal Karl Gerd von Rundstedt, the enemy attained tactical surprise, swiftly penetrated the lightly held Allied lines, and moved west thirty-five miles in the first three days. In the end, the Germans penetrated Allied territory more than fifty miles before they were stopped. Dubbed the Battle of the Bulge, this was Eisenhower's greatest challenge from the Germans in the European campaign.

Supply, fuel, and in particular, ammunition shortages slowed the Germans by the end of the first week of the battle. But, again, the heroism of the Allied troops turned the tide. Quickly redispersing his troops, Ike was able to launch an attack against the enemy's flank. Marshal Montgomery's forces struck in the north, and Patton's Third Army swung north, pressuring the southern German flank. Temporarily cutoff American units, such as those at Bastogne, fought bravely, delaying the German advance until Allied forces were able to penetrate to their positions.

At the end of two weeks, the German forces were essentially knocked out. The dark December was over. Under Allied pressure the enemy fell back toward the Rhine, the last natural barrier protecting Hitler's "Thousand-Year Reich." Hitler's counteroffensive had successfully delayed any offensive for perhaps six weeks. The cost, however, was enormous: over eighty thousand troops and hundreds of tanks, weapons, and aircraft—none of them replaceable. In the long run, Hitler's offensive had in fact hastened the reich's destruction and the end of the war.

What was left of German strength west of the Rhine slowly eroded. As the American forces reached that historic river, one of the great breaks of the war occurred: the American Ninth Armored Division was able to seize essentially intact the last remaining bridge over the Rhine at Remagen. Before the Lundendorff Bridge collapsed Eisenhower poured five divisions over it. The final battle for Germany was under way.

Events happened rapidly in April. The horror of the Nazi concentration camps was now apparent as camp after camp was overrun by the Allies. Roosevelt died on April 12, 1945, less than a month before the end of the war in Europe. On April 25 the American Sixty-ninth Division and a Soviet Guards division linked up on the Elbe River at Torgaù, only seventy-five miles south of Berlin. On April 30, Hitler committed suicide in his Berlin bunker. (Ike's old comrades in Italy had completed the occupation of all Italy to the Alps by May 6.)

On May 7, eleven months and one day after the landings in Normandy, the war ended in Eisenhower's headquarters, a little red schoolhouse in Reims, France. Field Marshal Alfred Jodl signed the instrument of surrender for the defeated Nazis. After tiring of his staff officers' efforts to write a grandiloquent message to the combined American and British chiefs of staff officially informing them of the surrender, Ike quickly wrote one in his own hand: "The mission of this allied force was fulfilled at 0241 local time, May 7, 1945." The Great Crusade was over.

Now the Europeans feted the victorious generals. Ike was not only an international figure but a household word as well. On June 10 Marshal Zhukov gave him the Soviet's highest award—the Order of Victory. In London two days later, millions cheered as he rode in an open carriage to the Guildhall, where he was granted the "freedom of the city." Then on June 14 a million Parisians cheered him in an elaborate ceremony at the Arc de Triomphe.

On June 18 he arrived at National Airport in Washington, D.C., to the shouts of "Ike, Ike!"; then he went on to Capitol Hill to address a joint session of Congress. The following morning he was in New York, where four million people greeted him as he rode through the streets of Manhattan. All of the attention was heady, but on Friday, June 22, he arrived at the place where the admiration meant the most and where it all began: Abilene, Kansas. Ida Eisenhower was there as well as his brothers. He had left Abilene in 1911 on a June day, a raw-boned boy from the great plains en route to West Point. On this June day 34 years later he was back—perhaps the best-known figure in the world that day.

Seven summers later Ike was to return to Abilene to embark on another crusade. In the meantime there were many tasks ahead for Ike, some in uniform, some out.

With Churchill and Major General
Maxwell D. Taylor, commander of the
101st Airborne Division (mid-May
1944).

American fighting men wade ashore under fire from Nazi machine guns.

After his appointment as supreme commander, Ike wrapped up affairs in Algiers and enjoyed a brief trip home in January 1944. He spent the time mostly in Washington with Mamie and took brief side trips to West Point to see John and to Kansas to visit his 82-year-old mother. By January 16 he was at work in London, and on the seventeenth he established Supreme Headquarters Allied Expeditionary Force (SHAEF). In this photo Ike is holding a Browning machine gun while visiting the troops (February 1944).

Observing armored maneuvers with Air Chief Sir Arthur Tedder and General Sir Bernard Montgomery somewhere in England (March 1944).

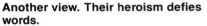
Another view. Their heroism defies words.

Germans erecting obstacles on the beaches in preparation for the Allied assault.

The evening before D-Day, Ike visited the 101st, the first American unit to touch down in Europe in the early morning hours of the Longest Day—June 6, 1944.

British Commandos land in the British sector.

Taking cover from direct fire.

Follow-up supplies to support the invading troops now ashore and established.

Secretary of the Navy James Forrestal (later the first secretary of defense) with Ike (August 1944).

In case the D-Day operations failed, Ike wrote this postdated note just before the invasion. He concealed it from others and kept it in his wallet.

Our landings in the Cherbourg — Havre area have failed to gain a satisfactory foothold and I have withdrawn the troops. This particular operation my decision to attack at this time and place was based upon the best information available. The troops, the air and the navy did all that Bravery and devotion to duty could do. If any blame or fault attaches to the attempt it is mine alone.

July 5

Ike confers with British Foreign Minister Anthony Eden on the progress of the campaign at Ike's field headquarters in France just before the liberation of Paris (August 21, 1944).

**Paris liberated! Ike with General
Bradley and French General Pierre
Joseph Koenig at the Arc de Triomphe,
shortly after the Allies had taken back
the City of Lights (August 26, 1944).**

Ike takes time for a cup of coffee while visiting the Eighth Infantry Division during operations against the German West Wall (November 9, 1944).

Talking to GIs during an inspection tour.

Visiting the Twelfth Evacuation Hospital, Ike autographs the leg cast of Private First Class John T. Dietz of Manchester, Connecticut.

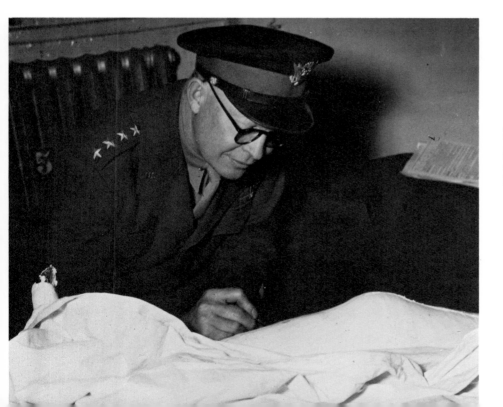

Ike poses informally with Bernard Montgomery, then commander of the 21st Army Group, and Omar Bradley who headed the Twelfth Army Group (fall 1944). The two commanders could not have been more different in temperament: Monty was flamboyant and temperamental, while Bradley was quiet and calm to the point of stoicism.

Ike had a steady stream of stateside visitors such as Congresswoman Clare Booth Luce from Connecticut who was also a member of the House Military Affairs Committee, which was then in France.

Dark December. At dawn on December 16, 1944, German infantry troops attacked on a seventy-five-mile wide front in the Ardennes Forest and penetrated Allied lines in what later became known as the Battle of the Bulge. At first the threat seemed serious, but the Allies beat the Germans back by the end of January. Shown are members of the U.S. 82nd Airborne Division moving through the snow somewhere in Belgium.

Infantrymen of the Third Armored Division advance under artillery fire in Pont-le-Ban, Belgium (January 15, 1945).

Upon entering Julich, Germany, the Twenty-ninth Division indicates its jubilation with this banner. The Allied forces had now penetrated the Thousand-Year Reich.

(March 2, 1945) Ike visits with Major General Charles H. Gerhardt, commander of the Twenty-ninth Division. Lieutenant General William Simpson, commander of the U.S. Ninth Army is in the background.

First Army infantrymen make their way through the rubble of Cologne, March 6, 1945.

In a rare and lucky break, an American unit seized the Ludendorff Bridge, which had been wired for detonation to prevent the Allies' easy access across the Rhine River. The unit ripped out the wires to save the bridge and eliminate the need for a bloody assault crossing. An American soldier views it from the German side (March 15, 1944).

The Allies began to take German prisoners on a large scale. The Seventh Army captured 11,000 prisoners when German resistance collapsed in the Saar and Palatinate areas.

Ike and Churchill visit Rhine crossing sites (March 1945). Note Bradley and General William Hood Simpson in the rear.

Ike and three of his field commanders —Patton, Bradley, and Courtney Hodges—meet briefly as the war nears its final stages. Patton was justifiably elated: his mighty Third Army was moving into the history books as one of the greatest western armies of all time. Patton, who dreamed of glory all his life, had achieved it, at last and forever.

Ike's major American commanders and staff officers pose with him in the spring of 1945. *Front row, left to right:* Lieutenant General William H. Simpson, Commanding General (C.G.) Ninth Army; General George S. Patton, C.G. Third Army; General Carl A. Spaatz, C.G. USSTAF; Eisenhower; General Omar N. Bradley, C.G. Twelfth Army Group; General Courtney H. Hodges, C.G. First Army; General Leonard T. Gerow, C.G. Fifteenth Army. *Back row, left to right:* General Ralph P. Sterling, C.G. Ninth Tactical Air Command (TAC); General Hoyt S. Vandenberg, C.G. Ninth Air Force; General W.B. Smith, chief of staff; General Otto P. Weyland, C.G. Nineteenth TAC; General Richard E. Nugent, C.G. Twenty-ninth TAC.

Ike holds a press conference at the Scribe Hotel in Paris (March 27, 1945). By now he had become adept at these.

The last great offensive of the war broke out of the Rhineland and across central Europe. A German SS trooper lies in the waters of the Schleuse River where he was shot by American troops as they drove on to Walsau, Germany (April 9, 1945).

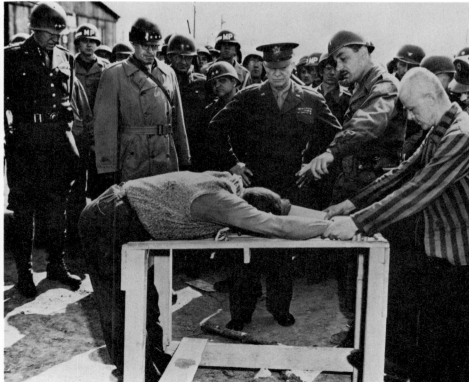

Holocaust horrors (April 12, 1945). Eisenhower impassively walks around a cluster of corpses in the Gotha, Germany, concentration camp. The inmates' bodies lie where they were slain by the Nazis in charge of the camp.

Ike watches grimly while surviving occupants demonstrate how they were tortured by their sadistic guards. Generals Patton and Bradley are at Ike's right.

The Yanks and Russians join hands on April 25. Patrols of the U.S. Sixty-ninth and Russian Fifty-eighth Divisions meet on the Elbe at Torgau, Germany, 75 miles south of Berlin.

Ike inspects German war booty— paintings, gold, silver, and paper currency—that was stored in a salt mine. Behind him are Bradley and Patton.

Ike announces Germany's unconditional surrender at SHAEF Headquarters in Reims, France, May 7, 1945, with his deputy Arthur Tedder at his side.

Bedell Smith, Ike's chief of staff, signs the unconditional surrender on behalf of the Allies at Reims, France. *On his right:* Admiral Harold M. Burrough, commander in chief of the Allied Naval Expeditionary Forces; *on his left:* Major General Ivan Susloporoff of the Russian artillery and General Carl Spaatz, head of the American strategic bombing of Germany.

Forgoing a grandiloquent message to the combined chiefs of staff officially informing them of the German surrender, Ike wrote a one-sentence note in his own hand.

Eisenhower and General Vassily Sokolovsk inspect Russian troops in Berlin (June 10, 1945).

Ike and Allied leaders drink a victory toast at his headquarters in Frankfurt.

Ike receives the ''Freedom of the City'' from London's Lord Mayor.

Eisenhower en route to the Guildhall, London, to make his famous speech (June 12, 1945).

In Washington, D.C., on June 18, 1945, Ike stands up in his car to wave to the thousands of happy Americans in front of the Capitol.

New York City. More than four million people thronged its streets and rained down tons of paper as Ike passed (June 19, 1945).

The parade Ike probably most enjoyed
was in Abilene (June 23, 1945). An
especially happy moment was when
his Abilene High School football squad
came down Third Street on a float.

**Back in Europe in August, Ike and
Soviet Marshal Georgi Zhukov tour
Leningrad. Ike was now commander of
the American Occupation Forces in
Germany.**

Road to the White House

With Presidents Truman and Hoover at
Princeton University's bicentennial
(June 17, 1947).

After the celebrations at home, Ike returned to Frankfurt, Germany, to the anticlimactic role of heading the American occupation zone and forces. In August 1945 he had the unusual experience, for a foreigner, of standing on Lenin's tomb next to Stalin as a huge sports parade marched by in Moscow's Red Square. Shortly before his visit to the Soviet Union came the surprise word that the United States had dropped the atomic bomb on Hiroshima. The announcement of Japan's surrender came the evening before Ike left Moscow.

For some time, Eisenhower had been mentioned as a presidential candidate, even though no one knew what party he favored. On one or two occasions President Harry Truman himself offered Ike the Democratic nomination. Ike declined. Still, he was not looking forward to his next job—replacing George Marshall as Army chief of staff the fall of 1945.

Normally, the chief of staff position would be the high point of an Army officer's career, but not in Ike's case. There had never been a job like that of supreme commander; no other military duty could match the demands of Operation Overlord. While Eisenhower did find challenges as Army chief of staff, they were not the types of problems that were truly solvable or that gave much satisfaction in trying.

The main task facing Ike was demobilization. Neither the service personnel nor their families shared the belief that the United States needed to maintain a major military force. The war was over, and the veterans wanted to return to their civilian pursuits. Eisenhower received a flood of mail, especially from parents who wanted their "boys" home. By the end of June 1947 when the demobilization officially ended, the American military force of twelve million at the war's end was down to 1.5 million. As President Truman said, this was disintegration, not demobilization.

Other problems intruded, too, particularly in reconverting to a peacetime economy. Amid inflation and tight budgets, Chief of Staff Eisenhower had to fight for the Army's slice of a very small pie. Another battle, over the future shape of the armed forces, was finally settled by the National Security Act of 1947. A Navy legislative victory, at first it called for a loose, federalized arrangement of the different services under a weak secretary of defense. Eisenhower and the Army had wanted instead a centralized defense establishment with a strong secretary of defense.

As if all this were not enough, the cold war began during Ike's years as chief of staff. One of its significant by-products was the Truman Doctrine of March 1947, leading to the U.S. policy of containment to check the expansion of communism. At the June 1947 Harvard commencement, Secretary of State George Marshall proposed a plan for the economic reconstruction of Western Europe, later known as the Marshall Plan.

Of course Ike was tremendously busy with all these concerns. He traveled widely and with Mamie, whenever possible. For every speech he made, he had to turn down forty others. In the eyes of most Americans he was a possible candidate for president. But for now he was still denying any interest.

More pleasant events were happening, too. In June 1947 John Eisenhower married Barbara Thompson, herself an "Army brat." The following March, Ike and Mamie became grandparents with the birth of a namesake, Dwight David Eisenhower II.

By the spring of 1947 Ike was becoming eager to leave active duty, but what would he do? It was too early for serious presidential campaigning, especially with Truman still in the running. Ike had lengthy discussions with Thomas J. Watson, chairman of the search committee for a successor to Nicholas Murray Butler, who had presided as president of Columbia University, New York, for fifty years. Meeting at West Point in June 1947, they agreed that Ike would become president of Columbia in about a year.

There was one other matter to resolve. Publishers were pressuring Ike for his memoirs of the war. Thus, in early February 1948, Ike turned over his duties as chief of staff to his successor General Omar Bradley. He returned to the seclusion of Fort Myer's Quarters One—the traditional home of the Army chief of staff—on terminal leave and wrote his first book, *Crusade in Europe*, in only three months. It was well received and made him a reasonably well-off man.

On the first Sunday in May 1948, he left Fort Myer and the Army for his first civilian home since 1911. He and Mamie settled in the house provided for the president of Columbia in Morningside Heights adjoining the New York City campus, a long way from Abilene. His formal induction took place at a convocation on October 12, 1948. Ike was now in a strange new world of trustees, deans, fund-raising, and public relations. All in all, although he was the butt of many of the professors' jokes, he handled himself well in this unfamiliar environment. In his thirty-two months at Columbia, he managed to juggle his duties at the university with an extraordinary amount of private political activity. As befit a potential presidential candidate, he met with Republican influentials. He was still connected with Washington, engaged in the spillover duties of a senior military figure and in helping the current administration.

When President Truman unexpectedly defeated Republican candidate Thomas Dewey in 1948, there was no question as to who was the long-range winner: Dwight Eisenhower. Had Dewey been elected, he might have been president for the next eight years. By then Ike would have been sixty-six and long out of the limelight. The Democratic victory therefore opened the doors to Ike as a Republican candidate in 1952.

The major international event during Ike's Columbia years was the Korean War. Shortly after North Korean communists invaded South Korea on June 25, 1950, Truman committed U.S. forces. By September, after early losses, they had made a brilliant comeback with MacArthur's end run at Inchon but were bogged down again when the Chinese intervened in November. The war, though a limited one, was to drag on for three years. Reserves were called up, and the economy suffered. In time the war became unpopular and so did Truman, who was unable to bring it to an end. That would play an important part in Eisenhower's 1952 election.

Of more immediate significance to Ike, however, were events in Europe set in motion by the Korean War. At first perceived as part of a worldwide communist offensive, the Korean War galvanized the North Atlantic Treaty Organization (NATO), which was organized in April 1949. In light of a succession of Soviet actions, especially the Czechoslovakian coup of February 1948 and the Berlin blockade of 1948–49, NATO members saw the need to establish a military infrastructure to guard against a Soviet attack in Europe. When NATO set up the military position of Supreme Allied Commander (SACEUR), what better person was there to turn to for the post than Eisenhower, the old wartime hero? It was not a bad place for a potential presidential candidate to be, either. Taking a leave of absence from Columbia, Ike took over his new command at Supreme Headquarters near Paris on January 7, 1951.

Eisenhower's SACEUR duties were more political than those of his wartime command. Among other things, he had to build support for a common defense among the twelve NATO nations, including his own. This meant that he had to deal with old national animosities as well as to convince the people of the NATO countries to believe in the cause and to put up their share of the money to support it.

Ike also used this time to refine and expand on the political contacts he had made during the Columbia years and to develop his own public position on international and domestic issues. Because of his experience, his internationalist views came naturally. Here he had a clear-cut edge over his chief rival in the Republican party, Senator Robert Taft. Ike's views on domestic matters were less developed, except for one certain and often-stated position: the strength and integrity of the American economy and financial structure must be preserved.

During the seventeen months that Ike was a chief player on the NATO stage, political prodding and prompting came at him from the wings to become an announced Republican candidate. Finally, in January 1952 he did acknowledge that he was a Republican. And he let Senator Henry Cabot Lodge enter his name in the New Hampshire presidential primary in March. When Ike won the primary, he was off and running.

On June 1, 1952, Ike left NATO and the military service to become an active candidate. While he began his campaign for the presidency with an undistinguished speech in Abilene, he retrieved it with an outstanding press conference the next day.

The July convention in Chicago made Eisenhower the Republican standard-bearer after tough going against Taft. Selecting Richard Milhous Nixon of California as his running mate soon turned into a dilemma for Ike with the disclosure that Nixon might have improperly accepted campaign money from businessmen. The vice–presidential candidate overcame the problem in his famous Checkers speech of September 23, 1952.

Other difficulties arose during Ike's whistle-stop campaign (he was the last president who campaigned extensively by train), especially when Senator Joseph McCarthy made some snide and false charges against Ike's old mentor George Marshall. Eisenhower's failure to defend Marshall was probably the nadir of his campaign. Its high point was the effectiveness of the three buzzwords with which the Republican candidate charged the Democrats: Korea, communism, and corruption. On October 24 in Detroit, he announced that after the election he would go to Korea, presumably to bring an end to the war. That was what the Americans wanted to hear, and from then on Ike was "in."

On election day, November 4, 1952, Dwight Eisenhower received 55 percent of the popular vote. The electoral vote gave him 442 against the 89 of his Democratic opponent, Adlai Stevenson. When Stevenson conceded in the early morning hours, one of Ike's first actions was to call former President Herbert Hoover, who was the last Republican to have held the job and had left the White House twenty years before during the Great Depression. The Republicans were back in the White House.

George Marshall returns from his frustrating mission to China, attempting to bring Chiang Kai-shek and Mao Tse-tung together, to report to President Truman. Ike meets him on his arrival in Washington (March 1946).

As Army chief of staff after World War II, Ike inherited demobilization problems, including mass demonstrations by the troops who wanted to be discharged. Here he testifies on the subject before the Congressional Affairs Committee (January 1946).

Ike visits his birthplace in Denison, Texas (April 1946).

The chief of staff relaxes during a stopover in Hawaii while on an extended inspection tour of the Pacific (May 1946).

During this period, Ike and Mamie visited Queen Elizabeth and King George at Balmoral Castle in Scotland. Also shown are John Eisenhower on the left and Princesses Margaret and Elizabeth on the right (October 6, 1946).

Somewhere in the British Isles. From the expression on Ike's face and the body language of the old gentleman behind him, Ike has just made a very good—or very bad—shot.

When Ike was chief of staff, he and Mamie had Quarters 1, Ft. Myer, Virginia, the traditional home of the Army chief of staff (1945–48).

Ike conducts a press conference aboard the White House yacht (April 1946). In the background is his aide Craig Cannon. Ike always enjoyed great rapport with reporters.

Atomic development and testing such as on the Bikini Atoll (July 25, 1946) continued apace after the war. Later when Ike was president, his overall military strategy had a heavy nuclear component.

Ike continued to be showered with honors. He receives an Honorary Doctor of Laws from the University of Edinburgh (October 3, 1946).

Ft. Monroe, Virginia, June 10, 1947. John Eisenhower married Barbara Thompson, who became the daughter Ike and Mamie never had.

Many portraits were made of Ike when he was chief of staff (November 1947). He particularly disliked this shot, though it shows an Ike—broadly grinning and cheerfully optimistic— that most Americans reacted to favorably.

In a news conference at the Pentagon (June 27, 1947), Ike told reporters he had "no political ambitions." Everyone, including Ike, had to smile.

Ike drops by a Columbia football practice to meet the team. The coach closest to Ike's left is Lou Little, whom Ike talked out of going to Yale (fall 1948).

Ike became Columbia University's president in May 1948. Here he and Mamie wave from the balcony of the president's house, 60 Morningside Drive, New York City.

Ike had many visitors at Columbia, mostly Republicans. A notable exception was Eleanor Roosevelt. Ike met her in his office before she delivered an address at the university (June 1948).

At its Convocation (October 12, 1948), Dwight Eisenhower was installed as Columbia University's president. Note Mamie and John looking on from left.

Ike on his inaugural day.

At the Books and Author's luncheon at the Hotel Astor in New York (November 23, 1948). Author Eisenhower *(Crusade in Europe)* talks with Irita Van Doren and Walter White as Burl Ives looks on.

In December Ike conferred with Secretary of Defense James Forrestal, who was to die tragically the following May as a direct result of the pressures of his job.

Grandchildren David and Anne in bed
with Ike and Mamie on New Year's Day
(1951). One of Ike's greatest pleasures
was spending time with his
grandchildren. They lived nearby with
their parents at West Point while John
was stationed at the Military Academy.

Ike and elder statesman Bernard
Baruch at the graduation exercises of
the Industrial College of the Armed
Forces, Ft. McNair, Washington, D.C.
(June 25, 1949).

THE WHITE HOUSE
WASHINGTON

December 19, 1950

Dear General Eisenhower:

The North Atlantic Treaty Nations have agreed on the defense organization for Europe and at their request I have designated you as Supreme Allied Commander, Europe. I view their request as a pledge that their support of your efforts will be complete and unequivocal.

I understand that the Standing Group of the North Atlantic Treaty Organization will shortly issue a directive to you concerning your responsibility and authority as the Supreme Allied Commander, Europe.

You are hereby assigned operational command, to the extent necessary for the accomplishment of your mission, of the U. S. Army Forces, Europe; U. S. Air Forces, Europe; and the U. S. Naval Forces, Eastern Atlantic and Mediterranean.

Subject to overriding requirements of the Supreme Allied Commander, Europe, the missions, routine employment, training and administration of these forces will continue to be handled through command channels heretofore existing.

You are authorized to have officers and enlisted personnel of the U. S. Armed Forces, as well as civilian employees of the Departments of the Army, Navy and Air Force, for your Staff in such numbers and grades as you consider necessary.

I am sending a copy of this letter to the Secretary of State for his guidance and a copy to the Secretary of Defense for his guidance and necessary action by the Department of Defense.

You are undertaking a tremendous responsibility. As President and Commander-in-Chief of the Armed Forces of the United States, I know that our entire country is wholeheartedly behind you. Indeed, you carry with you the prayers of all freedom-loving peoples. I send you my warmest personal good wishes for success in the great task which awaits you.

Very sincerely yours,

Harry Truman

General of the Army Dwight D. Eisenhower,
United States Army.

President Truman, seeing Ike off at the airport in Washington, D.C., as Ike leaves to take command of NATO. *Also shown:* Secretary of Defense George Marshall, Secretary of State Dean Acheson, and Major General Floyd Parks, Ike's public relations officer when he was chief of staff.

The outbreak of the Korean War galvanized the NATO countries to set up a military infrastructure and to appoint a supreme allied commander. Naturally NATO turned to Ike, the wartime commander, to take on the job, and Truman wrote a letter to Ike, making the appointment.

When told Truman had fired General MacArthur from his post as supreme commander in the Far East, Ike's face was far more eloquent than his response, ''Well, I'll be darned'' (April 1951).

Ike and Mamie on a visit to the United States (November 1951).

As Supreme Allied Commander of Europe, Ike ranked a palatial estate at Marnes-la-Coquette.

Ike and his chief of staff, General Alfred Gruenther leave Supreme Headquarters, Allied Powers Europe (SHAPE) in January 1952. Ike proved to be the perfect man to rally the desperate NATO-member nations to support the alliance.

In February 1952 Republicans, hoping to persuade Ike to be their candidate, held a rally in Madison Square Garden in New York with a cheering, placard-waving crowd of 15,000.

Finally Ike gave in. He asked Truman to place him on the inactive list as of June 1, 1952—the date Ike had previously agreed with his supporters that he should begin his campaign for the Republican presidential nomination.

D D E

Supreme Headquarters
Allied Powers Europe
2 April 1952

Dear Mr. Secretary:

I request that you initiate **appropriate action to secure my release from assignment as Supreme Commander, Allied Powers Europe,** by approximately **June 1st, and that I be placed** on inactive status upon my return to the **United States. A relief date** fixed this far in advance should **provide ample time for the appointment of a** successor and for any **preparation and counsel** that he may desire from me.

This proposal is in **the spirit of the understanding I gained from** officials in **Washington who outlined the special purposes of my** original appointment in **December 1950. At that** time it was believed by those **individuals that, because of past experience, I** had relationships with **respect to Europe which would facilitate the** formation of a common **defense structure and the establishment of** a pattern for its operation. **An assumption on the part of respon-** sible officials of our **Government that I could be helpful in the** vital task of preserving peace was, of course, a compelling rea- son for instantaneous return to active service and acceptance of this assignment.

As of now, I consider that the specific **purposes** for which I was recalled to duty have been largely accomplished; the command has been formed, its procedures established, and basic **questions** settled. Moreover, a program of growth and development, **based** on early experience and searching reexamination, has been **agreed** at governmental levels. There are many difficulties to be over- come but, given the wholehearted support of the NATO community, this program will provide a reassuring degree of security in this

region, despite the continued presence of the threat of Soviet Communism. There is every reason to believe that the NATO nations will continue to work together successfully, toward the goal of a secure peace.

Sincerely,

Dwight D. Eisenhower

The Honorable Robert A. Lovett
Secretary of Defense
Room 3E880, Pentagon
Washington 25, D. C.

In June he made a courtesy call on the president to report on the situation in Europe. *Also shown: left*, Secretary of Defense Robert A. Lovett and *right*, Secretary of the Army Frank Pace, Jr.

While Ike and Truman appear to be great friends, such was not the case. Truman's rancor toward Ike was to last the remainder of his life.

A candid shot catches Ike just as he has been told that Douglas MacArthur has been named the keynote speaker at the forthcoming Republican National Convention (June 10, 1952).

Ike opened his campaign in the rain at Abilene (June 7, 1952). The speech was a disaster, but he rebounded the next day with a great press conference.

Scenes at the convention (July 1952). This was the first national convention to be covered by television. While the battle between Ike and Robert Taft for the nomination was close for awhile, Ike ended up winning on the first ballot.

Ike (July 9, 1952) after defeating Taft.

The new ticket.

Taft congratulates Ike.

The party closes ranks behind their nominee.

Ike and Mamie at the American Legion Convention in Madison Square Garden (August 28, 1952).

Ike's nomination speech, in which he pledged to lead the Republican party to "total victory."

Taking a break from the rigors of politics. Ike had always been a cook on his boyhood outings, and he continued to enjoy camp cooking all his life. Here he makes a breakfast of flapjacks and bacon at a mountain retreat near Fraser, Colorado, in July 1952.

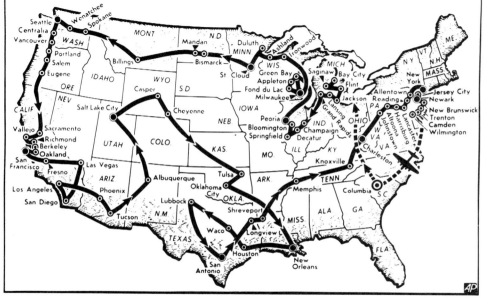

Candidate Eisenhower riding down famous Peachtree Street in Atlanta where he wooed the supposedly solidly Democratic South. And his work paid off. Though he did not carry Georgia, Ike did crack the Democratic hold, winning five southern states in the 1952 election.

A map showing Ike's campaign route across the country.

Ike and Mamie make an unplanned appearance at a whistle stop in Salisbury, North Carolina, during the campaign (September 26, 1952).

Ike and Mamie campaign in West Virginia (September 1952).

Ike meets Richard Nixon at Wheeling, West Virginia, the night after his running mate's famous Checkers speech. Ike has just told Nixon, "You're my boy" (September 24, 1952).

Ike's refusal to repudiate publicly Senator Joseph McCarthy of Wisconsin was highly controversial. Ike shakes McCarthy's hand on a visit to Milwaukee (October 1952).

Ike addresses a noon-hour throng in the garment district of New York City (October 30). The crowd stretched the six blocks from 35th to 41st Streets.

A key address at Madison Square Garden in October, when Ike told 20,000 people that the Democratic campaign being waged was just plain ''dirty.'' Mud-slinging was a new experience for the neophyte politician.

This time the *Chicago Tribune* got it right.

Ike and Mamie acknowledge his victory. After he received Stevenson's concession, Ike spoke over radio and on television.

Proudly holding a brace of pheasants. He made frequent visits to Secretary of the Treasury George Humphrey's plantation in Georgia, where the hunting was superb.

Ike and Mamie went to Augusta, Georgia, to rest for a few days, though of course the visitors continued. Governor Thomas Dewey came November 14 to give Ike ideas on his forthcoming trip to Korea; Dewey flatly denied he wanted to be in Ike's new cabinet.

Ike's golfing costume had improved considerably since Manila.

Senator Taft was a staunch supporter of Ike's policies in the Senate where he was majority leader the first two years of Eisenhower's presidency. Here they discuss party affairs (November 19, 1952).

Ike met with President Truman at the White House to discuss administrative changes prior to the changeover on January 20. The relationship between the two was now cool at best.

As he had promised, Ike went to Korea. Here he has chow with enlisted soldiers of the Fifteenth Infantry, U.S. Third Division. Behind him is Lieutenant General Reuben Jenkins, commander of the U.S. Ninth Corps.

Ike walks the line during a troop review ceremony of the Republic of Korea (ROK) Capitol Division.

Returning from Korea, Ike held budget and strategy sessions with future cabinet officers aboard the USS *Helena*.

In mid-December Ike met with his old
boss, Douglas MacArthur, to discuss
the Korean problem.

CHAPTER
7
Mr. President

January 20, 1953. From the north portico of the White House and up Pennsylvania Avenue rode the outgoing President Harry S Truman and the first Republican president in twenty years, Dwight David Eisenhower. Ike—buoyant, cheerful, sunny, and seemingly uncomplicated—was the ultimate folk hero of his time.

His short inaugural address was devoted mostly to foreign policy matters with only passing reference to domestic issues. The next day many newspapers noted that the speech was a repudiation of isolationism and furthermore was a message to the Taft wing of the Republican party: the party must revise its traditional isolationist views and relate more to a changing world.

In filling his cabinet posts Eisenhower tended toward wealthy businessmen. One exception was Martin Durkin, a labor union president (thus the quip that the cabinet consisted of "nine millionaires and a plumber"). Another who was not a businessman was John Foster Dulles, soon to become Ike's most famous cabinet member.

While Ike's selection of John Foster Dulles as secretary of state was not inevitable, it did not come as a surprise. Dulles, possessing considerable talents for the office, had worked long and hard for it, spending most of his career as a highly successful Wall Street lawyer specializing in international cases. In 1944 he became presidential candidate Thomas Dewey's chief adviser on foreign policy and from then on was associated with government. At the 1945 United Nations Conference in San Francisco, he became involved in diplomatic practice, and by the late 1940s, Dulles was the unofficial foreign policy spokesman for the Republican party. When Dewey's defeat in 1948 cost Dulles the secretary of state job, the Truman administration, in efforts at a bipartisan foreign policy, employed him extensively. Everyone knew Dulles's views on foreign affairs and how strongly they were linked with his perception of the communist threat.

During Ike's first two years in office, the Republicans had a majority in Congress, but it was so small the administration was forced to seek Democratic backing to implement its programs. To bring Congress around to his point of view, Eisenhower used his considerable abilities of persuasion and compromise. This was good practice for what was to come, since the Eighty-fourth Congress was the only Congress of the four during Ike's presidency that was Republican-controlled.

About six weeks after Eisenhower's inauguration, Stalin died. Washington speculated as to who would replace him and whether the death of the old tyrant would improve relations between the United States and the Soviet Union. No one could know, but it was time for deeds rather than words, and Ike soon put forth some spectacular foreign initiatives.

First came what has been cited as the finest speech of his presidency. Entitled "The Chance for Peace," Ike gave it before the American Society of Newspaper Editors on April 16, 1953. Here was a former general of the army stating that "the cost of one heavy bomber is a modern brick school in more than thirty cities" or "two fine, fully equipped hospitals." He then aimed some proposals directly at the Kremlin that would, if carried out, presumably turn bombers into schools and hospitals. In effect, he was asking if the Soviets were ready to negotiate agreements for controlling atomic energy and prohibiting atomic weapons. Coming when it did, his proposals were startling, but for the moment no Soviet leadership was in place to pick up the offer.

More immediate results came from his other initiative: achieving a truce in the Korean War that had been waged since June 1950. In the campaign Ike had promised that if he were elected he would end the war in Korea; now it was time for action. To hasten the end of the interminable armistice talks, which had been conducted with the communists since June 1951, Ike let it be known through Dulles that the United States was not willing to tolerate much more stalling. The Chinese, who had entered the war in the fall of 1950, were told that Manchuria would be considered enemy territory if the stalemate continued. There was also an implicit threat that if necessary Ike would employ atomic weapons to end the war.

Whether the threat worked or the armistice was an event whose time had come, the agreement was concluded. At 10:00 P.M. Korean local time, July 27, 1953, all action ceased. Ending the killing in Korea was one of Dwight Eisenhower's greatest achievements.

But another war drew America into Asia. Complex and seemingly endless, the French–Vietnamese struggle in Indochina was in its seventh year when Ike took office. The United States had gotten involved in early 1950 by giving substantial military aid to the French who were then making an all-out effort to retain their colony. As the war dragged on, however, the French home front became less and less supportive of this colonial adventure.

In early 1954 the French got themselves in a pickle when their troops were surrounded at Dien Bien Phu. France asked for American help—perhaps atomic weapons or, at least, conventional bombers. Ike knew that the former was out of the question, and that it was already too late to use bombers. Further, he had no intention of getting U.S. forces involved. Ike responded with impossible conditions for American intervention: congressional support—which he knew he would not get—and British support. Since the British were dismantling their own colonial empire, they certainly would not aid the French in keeping theirs. Ike kept demurring, and the French fortress fell on May 7, 1954.

The day after Dien Bien Phu fell, the two opponents began a conference in Geneva about the future of Vietnam. On July 21 the truce was signed, temporarily dividing Vietnam at the seventeenth parallel. Ike kept the United States out of that war in 1954 but did not extricate America from the quagmire that he later took over from the French. The Vietnam struggle would, after his presidency, become the longest and only lost U.S. war.

On February 9, 1950, Senator Joseph McCarthy claimed to have a list of communists in the State Department, thus starting a protracted political struggle in Eisenhower's party. McCarthy's claims turned out to be fiction, but meanwhile he set off a wild witch hunt in the government. Already widespread when Ike was elected, what was known as the McCarthy era lasted until late 1954 when McCarthy lost the chairmanship of his investigative committee and the Senate soon voted to censure him.

Ike, feeling the best way to suppress McCarthy was to ignore him, refused to confront his fellow Republican directly. But he did take indirect swipes at McCarthy during press conferences and on other occasions. Ike thought the Senate should handle the McCarthy problem, and it did so eventually. But in the meantime, people in many walks of life had their reputations and livelihoods perniciously ruined by the junior senator from Wisconsin. While Ike's handling of the McCarthy affair was not the president's greatest moment, in the end, McCarthy did as Ike had predicted: he destroyed himself.

In July 1955 Eisenhower went to Geneva for the first summit conference since the end of World War II. Nicolai Bulganin, the Soviet premier, and Nikita Khrushchev, then the new boss of the Communist party, represented the Soviets.

Eisenhower proposed the "open skies" plan in which the United States and the Soviet Union would furnish blueprints of each other's military establishments. This would include the right to take aerial photographs over each other's territories (satellites were not yet in operation). In sum, Ike thought the plan was one way to relax tensions about surprise attacks. The startled Russians said nothing of substance. Thus the summit turned out to be more show business than achievement, but it was at least a step in the right direction.

Two months later, Ike was off to Denver, Colorado, for a "work and play" vacation. On Tuesday, September 23, after a game of golf, he had retired early at the home of Mamie's parents. In the middle of the night, he awoke with chest pains and was immediately attended by his personal physician, General Howard Snyder. The president was having a heart attack, and by Saturday morning he was in Fitzsimons Army Hospital. Trading on the New York Stock Exchange that Monday reflected the nation's shock and concern with the heaviest losses the exchange had ever registered.

Vice President Nixon took over in a discreet way at cabinet and National Security Council meetings. Prior to the attack, the question of presidential disability had never arisen, but soon Ike was seeing officials and reading state papers. His chief of staff, the laconic Sherman Adams, functioned as Ike's liaison officer in Denver, and on public matters Jim Hagerty, his tough and skilled public relations man, took charge. On Friday, November 11, the president walked out of Fitzsimons Hospital and was flown back to Washington. With the well wishes of the country, Ike was back in charge.

The next year, 1956, was a presidential election year. Before long Ike was involved in the campaign. Adlai Stevenson, again the Democratic candidate, was never able to mount a serious challenge to Eisenhower. On matters of foreign policy, Ike's image was particularly strong. The French and British attack on Egypt and the uprisings in Hungary and Poland dominated the news during the final part of the campaign. As a result, the public's attention was focused on international crises. It was a poor time for Stevenson and the Democratic party to appeal for a change of presidents. Eisenhower's image was strong on domestic issues as well; the relative prosperity of his first administration had done much to erase the association of a Republican presidency with a depression, the legacy of Hoover's time. Ike's disposition to accept, and in mild ways to extend, the social welfare policies of FDR's New Deal and the Fair Deal also stole some Democratic thunder on domestic issues.

The election was an overwhelming personal victory for Dwight Eisenhower: 457 electoral votes for him to Stevenson's 73. Unfortunately, despite Ike's victory, the Republicans were unable to carry either house of Congress; that had not happened in over one hundred years. Ike, however, had been accustomed to working with a Congress controlled by the opposition party since 1952 when his administration and the Eighty-fourth Congress had worked together quite harmoniously. After the 1956 elections, the good working relationships between the conservative president and the liberal congressional leaders—Lyndon Johnson in the Senate and Sam Rayburn in the House—continued until the latter part of 1959, when preliminary activities for the 1960 presidential election began.

In the reviewing stand for the inaugural parade Ike stands behind his grandchildren Barbara Anne and David, while Richard Nixon is behind daughters Julie and Tricia. David gazes admiringly at Julie's beautiful black eye. The two were to marry 15 years later.

Dwight D. Eisenhower being sworn in
as the thirty-fourth president of the
United States (January 20, 1953). Chief
Justice Fred M. Vinson administers the
oath of office. Ike's inaugural address
was comparatively short and was
directed almost exclusively to foreign
policy matters.

Note the simplicity and smallness of the reviewing stand compared to extravagant inaugural celebrations in the 1980s.

Ike's first news conference as president (February 17, 1953). His sometimes garbled syntax became a symbol of ineptitude for his detractors, but Ike, a past master at the precise use of language, knew what he was doing. Sometimes it was best not to speak too clearly.

Secretary of Defense ''Engine'' Charlie Wilson hosted a luncheon for Ike at the Pentagon. Also attending were the service secretaries and Joint Chiefs of Staff, both present and designate.

Ike's face, always expressive, conveyed his thoughts as well as his emotions.

FDR first used Camp David, the presidential retreat in Maryland, and called it Shangri-La. Ike renamed the retreat after his grandson David, the name by which it is still known in 1990. It continues to be a favorite of incumbent presidents for its comfort, beauty, and seclusion. Ike often hosted important visitors here, such as Nikita Khrushchev in September 1959.

Ike prepares to address the United Nations (December 8, 1953). This was to be his famous "Atoms for Peace" speech, which received an enormous ovation from the UN delegates.

General Paul Ely, chairman of the French Joint Chiefs, flew to Washington to ask for American help for the besieged French forces at Dien Bien Phu (March 22, 1954). Ike said no. With the president and Ely is Chairman of the Joint Chiefs Admiral Arthur Radford.

Viet Minh troops hoist their flag over French Commander de Castrie's bunker (May 7, 1954). The final French radio transmission was sent shortly before: "Fini, fini, fini."

Secretary of Welfare Oveta Culp
Hobby, the only woman in Ike's
cabinet. A prominent newspaper
publisher from Houston, she had been
one of the Texas ''Democrats for
Eisenhower'' who had helped Ike get
elected.

Ike at a news conference (July 21,
1954), announcing the United States's
refusal to sign the Geneva Accords
that ended the French war in
Indochina. However, U.S. assistance to
the state being set up in the south was
planned.

David Eisenhower at age five gives a courtly greeting to his grandfather on the golf course at Augusta, Georgia.

Ike took great delight in showing visitors around his farm at Gettysburg, especially the livestock he had acquired. As he said, "I love animals. I like to go out and see them."

Ike and Nikolai Bulganin, chairman of the Council of Ministers of the USSR, at the Geneva Conference (July 1955). This was the first summit meeting since World War II and included the heads of the United States, the Soviet Union, Great Britain, and France.

Ike and Dulles at the Geneva Conference.

Ike and Mamie had given David a set of miniature golf clubs. Here are grandfather and grandson on vacation in Colorado in August 1955.

On October 25, 1955, Ike suffered a heart attack while vacationing in Denver. In his first pictures at Fitzsimons Army Hospital, Ike wears red pajamas with a flower-bedecked tie. Note the embroidered ''much better thanks'' and the sixth star, which had been given him by his doctor, Paul Dudley White, for ''good conduct.''

Ike announces he would be willing to run for reelection (February 29, 1956).

"How Do You Do"

Political cartoonist Herblock enjoyed portraying Ike as a laid back, golf-playing president who let things drift in foreign affairs. He may even have believed it. Many did, until the historical record was declassified and evidence showed that in foreign matters Ike was a strong, active, and effective president.

From HERBLOCK'S SPECIAL FOR TODAY (Simon & Schuster, 1958).

Assistant to the President Sherman Adams and Ike vacationing in New Hampshire (June 1955). Adams was Ike's able chief of staff and served his boss efficiently until he was forced to resign September 22, 1958.

Ike getting ready for a press conference with his tough and capable Press Secretary Jim Hagerty.

Ike being asked by a reporter if he was going to choose Nixon as his running mate again. Ike replied that he would be very happy to run for re-election with Vice President Nixon (March 14, 1956).

Ike throws out the first ball opening
the 1956 baseball season. *At right:*
Yankee Manager Casey Stengel.

Herblock portrays one version of Ike's relationship with the Republican National Committee (August 1956).

"You Came Here Your Very Self!"

From HERBLOCK'S SPECIAL FOR TODAY (Simon & Schuster, 1958).

Secretary of State John Foster Dulles reporting to the nation on his talks with the British and French leaders regarding the Egyptian seizure of the Suez Canal (August 3, 1956). Dulles became known for his references "for going to the brink." In fact, Ike was in charge of American foreign policy, and Ike kept both Dulles and the United States away from the brink.

Scenes from the Republican National Convention (August 1956).

A popular First Lady, Mamie greets the crowd at the Convention in San Francisco (August 22).

Ike at the podium giving his famous V for Victory salute.

Here with his running mate, Vice President Nixon.

Adlai Stevenson was once again Ike's Democratic opponent. As to grins, it was a pretty close race, but not the election. Ike won the popular vote by ten million, double the margin of his 1952 victory.

Election night (November 6, 1956). *From left:* John Eisenhower, Mrs. Doud, Ike, Mamie, Pat Nixon, and Richard Nixon.

The victors.

CHAPTER 8

Waging Peace

President Eisenhower points to Berlin
on a map of Germany before
addressing the American people on
the Berlin crisis. In his televised
speech, the chief executive expressed
his willingness to negotiate with the
Soviets. In the end, Ike and
Khrushchev held a summit rather than
a war (March 16, 1959).

Eisenhower's second presidential term and final public service offered extraordinary challenges and opportunities, particularly from mid–1957 until the end of 1958. Bringing to bear all his remarkable experience of a half-century, he drew on his talents—poise, introspection, balanced judgment, and decisiveness—to meet the challenges.

One of the most difficult domestic issues facing the nation was the desegregation of Little Rock schools. In September 1957 a confrontation with Arkansas Governor Orval Faubus ended with a presidential order to send federal troops to effect desegregation. Ike thought he had handled the matter decisively, but inevitably on this and other civil rights issues, he was criticized for lack of presidential leadership. This criticism was especially directed toward his failure to speak out against segregation by showing personal approval of the *Brown v. Topeka* ruling. Yet Ike always felt that to go further than he did would have produced a violent resistance in the South and, furthermore, that the president should never address Supreme Court decisions.

The state of the American economy was another domestic problem. While Eisenhower's administration had weathered the recession of 1953–54 fairly well, the one that began in October 1957 was a sterner test. In February 1958, unemployment more than doubled to 7.7 percent of the labor force. From the administration's point of view, however, the chief threat was inflation, thus fiscal remedies could not feed inflationary forces. In particular, Ike's advisers wanted to avoid a massive public works program and a tax cut. Eventually, the economy recovered, but the Republican party was to pay the price for the recession in the 1958 congressional elections.

Still, Ike received high marks for eight years of prosperity marred only by the two short recessions. His fiscal policies, particularly his insistence in at least trying to balance the budget, played a key role in the overall healthy economy of the 1950s.

Eisenhower's greatest tests and successes in his second term came on the international scene. The most dramatic of these—a kind of psychological challenge—came when the Soviet satellite Sputnik orbited in October 1957. The blow was two-fisted: it knocked over the image of American technological superiority, and U.S. citizens feared that for the first time their homeland was vulnerable to Soviet intercontinental missiles. The public and Congress clamored for the commitment of national resources to regaining technological superiority. From Ike's point of view, the United States had never really lost it; as future events showed, he was correct.

Some changes in the budget were inevitable, but Ike kept it in balance. Seeking approval for his prudent approach, he resorted to television, giving "confidence speeches" to help counter public anxiety over the Soviet feat. Two of his talks stressed that the overall strength of the free world was greater than that of the communist countries and that the United States must be selective in expending its resources. Nevertheless, the notion of a "missile gap" that was invented by the Democrats during this period survived as an issue in the 1960 presidential campaign.

Ike's planned third speech on the Sputnik controversy was overtaken by personal physical events. In his office on November 25, 1957, he suddenly felt dizzy and became orally incoherent. He was having a mild stroke. His condition soon improved, but symptoms remained for several days. This situation bothered Ike in a way that his previous two presidential illnesses had not. (Besides the 1955 heart attack, he had an emergency operation for ileitis in 1956.) Now sixty-seven years old, he worried about presidential disability and therefore arranged with Richard Nixon just how the vice president would take over if Ike were incapacitated. No one wanted a repeat of Woodrow Wilson's last year and a half as an invalid president in the White House.

The 1958 congressional elections were a disaster for Ike's party. Added to the recession and other uneasy matters such as Sputnik was a White House scandal. In the summer of 1958 Eisenhower tried to defend his Chief of Staff Sherman Adams, on whom he depended greatly, against charges that Adams had accepted some gifts from Boston industrialist Bernard Goldfine. The implication that Adams had used his position to do favors for Goldfine was never proved, but Adams finally had to resign. The outcome of the 1958 election substantially increased the Democrats' hold on both the Senate and the House.

Also in November 1958, Nikita Khrushchev initiated a crisis over Berlin. Since the end of World War II, the German city had been a crunch point for the Soviets to apply pressure on the West. The Soviets sent an ultimatum to the other three occupying powers (Great Britain, France, and the United States) and the Federal Republic of Germany, demanding that negotiations over Berlin's becoming a "free city" had to be productive within six months; if not, the Soviets would block access to the city. The note also warned that aggressive action against any member of the Warsaw Pact would be cause for appropriate action. Eisenhower's people huddled to confront the crisis. One military proposal was to force the issue with large Allied ground forces if necessary. Ike said no; a token force would do. If it did not, there would be time to issue his own ultimatum—nuclear war. In the end, the crisis passed, and Khrushchev and Ike had a summit rather than a war.

Secretary of State John Foster Dulles had become very close to Ike in the presidential years. He had not slowed down his activities even after the first signs of terminal cancer appeared in 1956. But in April 1959 Dulles was incapacitated by the disease and died the following month. This great personal loss for the president also marked the emergence of Ike as his own public secretary of state. (Actually he had always called the shots, though generally Dulles articulated them publicly.) Eisenhower began to travel and to hold a series of meetings with heads of state.

The most spectacular events of this new diplomacy focused on Nikita Khrushchev. For various reasons, Ike felt it expedient to invite the Soviet leader to the United States, and at a press conference on August 5, 1959, the president announced the premier's forthcoming visit. While some American allies applauded, others did not. To help ease their anxiety, Ike visited Bonn, London, and Paris. This successful trip in the summer of 1959 brought out enormous, welcoming crowds in all three capitals.

On September 15 Khrushchev boarded his plane for the United States with his own mission—promoting himself. American officials did not realize it at the time, but Khrushchev's personal position in the Soviet was weak. He needed to develop his image as a world figure, well known and liked even in America.

His trip began with a cross-country tour to California then a return to the East Coast. Khrushchev proved to be one of a kind, alternately blunt, clever, humorous, and tough. Even Hollywood was no match for him. His U.S. tour ended with private meetings with Ike at Camp David, where nothing much was settled except that Eisenhower would visit the Soviet Union in 1960 after a May summit in Paris between Khrushchev and allied leaders. As for Khrushchev's personal mission, the enormous hoopla and publicity attending his every appearance was just what he wanted.

In December, the president went on a triumphal tour of eleven countries: Italy, Turkey, Pakistan, Afghanistan, India, Iran, Greece, Tunisia, France, Spain, and Morocco—twenty-two thousand miles in nineteen days! The huge outpouring of people to see him in every country was phenomenal. A shorter trip in February 1960 to Latin America again attracted warm crowds, though punctuated with occasional shouts against "Yankee imperialism." All in all, Ike's program of personal diplomacy looked rosy as he entered his final year in office, and he looked forward to the May summit with Khrushchev. Then came the U-2 incident.

In the early morning of May 1, 1960, a U-2 plane piloted by Francis Gary Powers took off from Peshawar, Pakistan, on a photographic espionage mission covering three thousand miles of the Soviet Union. Though neither the American nor the Russian people knew of these missions, which had been going on for about four years, the Soviet government was well aware of them. Before, the Soviets had not been able to destroy them, but by the May flight they could. The plane was shot down, with the pilot captured alive and relatively unhurt. The Soviets, however, did not reveal that they had the pilot.

The United States immediately issued a cover story that the pilot had gone off course and inadvertently strayed over the Soviet Union. Then Khrushchev produced the pilot, who told all. The subsequent embarrassment to the United States was not the only fallout of this event. For the first time, many Americans felt a distrust of their own government's pronouncements. To Ike's credit, he insisted on accepting complete responsibility. He pointed out that all nations conducted espionage within their capabilities. Ike was to say later, "The big error we made, of course, was in the issuance of a premature and erroneous cover story. Allowing myself to be persuaded on this score is my principal personal regret."

The real impact of the U-2 incident came about a week later when the previously scheduled summit convened at Paris with Khrushchev, French President de Gaulle, British Prime Minister Harold Macmillan, and Eisenhower attending. In short order the Soviet chairman terminated the summit with a shouted tirade against the United States, culminating with the withdrawal of his invitation to Ike for a Moscow visit. This effectively terminated Ike's public diplomacy phase since the Japanese government canceled his trip to Japan scheduled for the following month because of mass demonstrations. The protests were not against Ike so much as against the Security Treaty between Japan and the United States then up for renewal.

An additional international matter, close at home, captured Eisenhower's attention during his final months in office and was later to plague his successor's first spring in the White House: Cuba.

Fidel Castro's takeover in Havana in January 1959 had received much popular support in the United States at first, but all this changed when his new government moved into the communist hegemony. By the end of 1959 Castro portrayed the United States as an enemy of the Cuban revolution. Ike finally became fed up with Castro's anti-Americanism and communist involvement. In March 1960, he approved a CIA recommendation to form, under that agency's control, a force of Cuban exiles for possible military use against Castro. How the force would be employed was not clear, but initially the CIA called for guerrilla operations. By the time of the American elections in November 1960, the idea had evolved into an invasion of Cuba, employing a brigade-sized force of exiles being trained secretly in Guatemala.

In one of his last diplomatic initiatives in early 1961 Ike severed relations with the Castro government. Thus his Cuban legacy to the new administration was (in the words of Kennedy-insider Arthur Schlesinger) "a force of Cuban exiles under American training in Guatemala, a committee of Cuban politicians under American control in Florida," and a CIA plan for these exiles to invade Cuba and to install the committee as the provisional government of Cuba. Whether Ike would have employed them in the ineffective manner that his successor did—or whether he would have employed them at all—is doubtful.

Ike's final six months in the White House were to some extent overshadowed by the 1960 campaign between John F. Kennedy and Richard Nixon. Eisenhower's campaigning for Nixon in late September was not enough to tip the scales in Nixon's favor. Kennedy won the presidency, though by the narrowest of margins. While the election was a great disappointment to Ike, the Republicans' loss did not diminish the enormous accomplishments of his eight years in the White House.

On the evening of January 17, 1961, Eisenhower addressed the nation for the last time as president. His farewell speech contained a warning that was to be remembered and restated for the remainder of the Eisenhower century and gave the language a new and indelible phrase: "the military-industrial complex." This heartfelt admonition was especially surprising coming from an old soldier:

> The conjunction of an immense military establishment and a large arms industry is new in the American experience. The total influence—economic, political, even spiritual—is felt in every city, every statehouse, every office of the federal government.
>
> In the councils of government, we must guard against acquisition of unwarranted influence, whether sought or unsought, by the military-industrial complex. The potential for the disastrous rise of misplaced power exists and will persist.
>
> We must never let the weight of this combination endanger our liberties or democratic processes.

Ike and James Hagerty prior to the president's May 14, 1957, address to the nation on the budget. Ike was a genuine conservative fiscally.

Ike asks a joint session of Congress for authority to use American forces in the Middle East if necessary. Behind him are Vice President Nixon and House Speaker Sam Rayburn (January 5, 1957).

Ike was presented the George Washington Carver Memorial Institute's Gold Medal for 1956 for his "outstanding contribution to the betterment of race relations and human welfare." *To Ike's right:* Dr. T.R.M. Howard, president of the National Medical Association; and Dr. William P. Tolley, chancellor of Syracuse University (January 5, 1957).

Eisenhower and Nixon toast each other while watching their second inaugural parade from the reviewing stand in front of the White House (January 21, 1957).

A 1942 Cadillac had been Ike's staff car in London when he was European Theater of Operations (ETO) commander and was photographed at the White House en route to the Eisenhower Museum in Abilene. With Ike is Master Sergeant Leonard Dry, formerly his driver and now Mrs. Eisenhower's chauffeur.

(May 8, 1957) Ike greets Ngo Dinh Diem, the first president of the Republic of Vietnam and whom the Eisenhower administration helped place in office. Until the early 1960s, he was an effective president and an uncompromising anticommunist. He was killed in a coup, supported by the Kennedy administration, on November 1, 1963.

British Prime Minister Harold Macmillan and Ike met in Bermuda (March 1957) to discuss British defense planning. Under the hat is Bermuda's governor Lieutenant General John Woodall.

Queen Elizabeth came to call at the
White House. She and Prince Phillip
made a state visit to the United States
October 19 and 20, 1957.

One of Ike's more pleasant
presidential duties was to open the
baseball season with its first pitch. He
and Vice President Nixon attend the
game between the Washington
Senators and Baltimore Orioles (1957).

Ike addresses newsmen at a hastily called press conference in his office. He told reporters he was prepared to call Congress into special session if it did not pass a foreign aid bill sufficient to meet national security requirements (August 14, 1957).

Ike presents the Distinguished Service Medal to retiring Joint Chiefs of Staff Chairman Admiral Arthur Radford, who saw eye-to-eye with the president on Ike's "New Look" strategy. Radford is one of the most powerful chairmen to have held that office in its forty-year history.

One of Ike's proudest moments: he signs the Civil Rights Bill while at the Summer White House in Newport, Rhode Island (September 9, 1957).

Less than a week after signing the civil rights legislation, Ike met with Governor Orval Faubus of Arkansas in an attempt to solve the Little Rock school desegregation controversy. Eventually Ike had to send in federal troops to uphold the law. The two emerge from their meeting (September 14, 1957).

At the height of the European post-Sputnik apprehension, the fifteen NATO governments convened in a ''parley at the summit'' in the Palais de Chaillot in Paris (December 16, 1957).

When the Soviets orbited Sputnik in October 1957, Ike took it in stride. In his drawing, Herblock depicts the pundits' conventional wisdom that the president was too complacent. In fact Ike was fully aware of the many classified programs the United States had in motion that would far surpass Soviet space efforts. Still it was unsettling to know that for the first time in its history the United States was vulnerable to an enemy missile attack.

HERBLOCK
©1957 THE WASHINGTON POST CO.

From HERBLOCK'S SPECIAL FOR TODAY (Simon & Schuster, 1958).

Ike in a March 26, 1958, news conference announcing that the nation is near the bottom of the recession and repeating his firm stand that he would not be panicked into proposing a tax cut. This was the second of two recessions during Ike's eight years in the White House.

President Eisenhower addresses over 200 Congressional Medal of Honor winners in the White House Rose Garden. They were in Washington to take part in a Memorial Day ceremony at Arlington National Cemetery during which unknown soldiers from World War II and the Korean War were laid to rest and also presented with Medals of Honor (May 30, 1958).

Ike sent troops into Lebanon in the summer of 1958. They did not see any action, which is better depicted by the Coca Cola stand rather than the troops behind the sandbags.

Ike poses with black leaders with whom he had been discussing civil rights issues. Present were Martin Luther King, Jr.; F. Frederic Morrow; Philip Randolph; William Rogers; and Roy Wilkins (June 23, 1958).

Mamie, Ike, John, Barbara, and the grandchildren on the presidential yacht *Barbara Anne,* named after the granddaughter standing on Ike's right. John and Mamie hold Mary Jean, while Susie stands in front of her mother seriously sucking her thumb and David looks on contemplatively.

President Eisenhower congratulates Alaska's Governor Mike Stepovitch on the Senate passage of the Alaska Statehood Bill. *At right:* Secretary of the Interior Fred Seaton holding a copy of the *Anchorage Daily Times* trumpeting, ''We're in!'' (July 1, 1958).

The First Family at the White House (Christmas 1958).

The baby boom was a part of Ike's presidency; large families were in vogue in the fifties. Here the president lifts two-year-old Steven Levelsmier of Carbondale, Illinois, into his chair at the White House during a ceremony in which Ike presented the forty-millionth copy of the government's best-seller, *Infant Care,* to Steven's parents, representing the American mother and father (October 16, 1958).

Ike meeting with legislative leaders (March 6, 1959).

Hawaii also became a state during Ike's presidency. Ike has just signed into law the bill making it the fiftieth state (March 18, 1959).

Ike and Churchill visit John Foster Dulles in Walter Reed Army Hospital where the latter was being treated for cancer. When he resigned in April 1959, he was replaced by Christian Herter. Dulles died on May 24, 1959.

King Hussein came to see Ike and strengthen relations between the United States and Jordan (March 25, 1959).

Secretary of State Herter gives Ike a firsthand report on the deadlocked Geneva Foreign Ministers' Conference and the rocky road to the summit (June 22, 1959).

The famous ''Kitchen Debate'' between Vice President Nixon and Premier Nikita Khrushchev at the U.S. exhibition at Sokolniki Park.

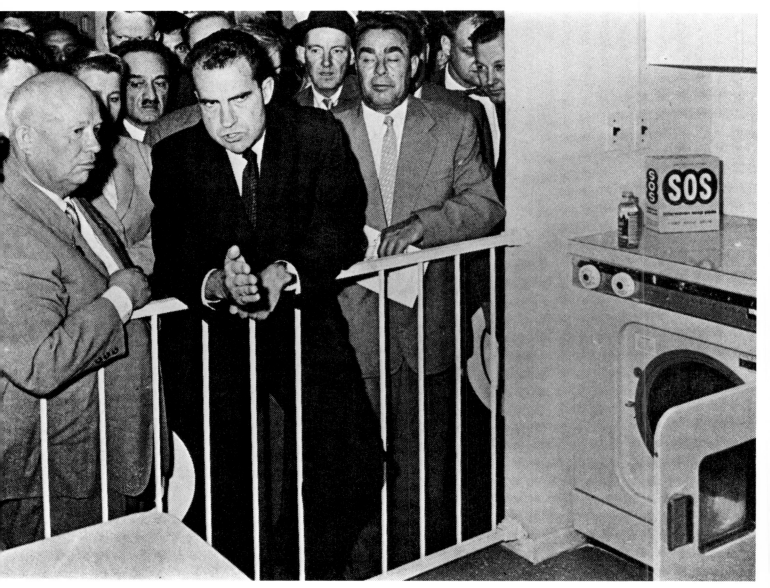

The Khrushchevs visited the United
States September 15, 1959, and were
feted at a state dinner at the White
House.

**Premier Khrushchev and President
Eisenhower met at Camp David at the
end of Khrushchev's U.S. tour
(September 25, 1959).**

**Meeting with the Pope in Rome. Also
present are interpreter Vernon Walters
and Ike's daughter-in-law Barbara
Eisenhower, who stood in for Mamie
on the trip (December 1957).**

In Karachi, Pakistan, with President Ayub Khan after Ike spoke to massed throngs.

Scenes from Ike's December 1957 personal diplomacy tour.

He addressed a crowd of over one-half million people in New Delhi.

Here he waves from an open car in Casablanca, Morocco, with King Mohammed.

In Paris Ike met with Macmillan, de Gaulle, and West German Chancellor Konrad Adenauer at a Western Big Four conference.

Discussing nuclear test negotiations with British Prime Minister Macmillan at Camp David (March 28, 1960).

He greets Mamie heartily on his return at Andrews Air Force Base (December 22). Looking on are Vice President Nixon and daughter-in-law Barbara.

He kept up assiduously with progress on missile development. With him is Major General Donald Yates, commander of the Cape Canaveral Missile Test Center (February 10, 1960).

Having discovered the jet's usefulness on his December trip, Ike set off on a goodwill tour of Latin America on February 22, 1960, to the four southernmost countries of the region. The motorcade drove through Rio, Brazil, with President Juscelino Kubitschek (February 24, 1960).

On April 20, 1960, Ike took a short holiday at Camp David. The next day, the U-2 incident occurred.

Khrushchev inspecting equipment from Francis Gary Powers's downed plane (1960).

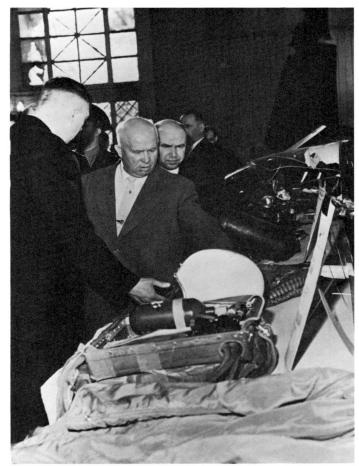

Ike ponders a reporter's question during the aftermath of the U-2 affair.

Ike's final goodwill trip as president (those planned for Moscow and Tokyo had both been canceled for different reasons) took him to the Philippines, Formosa, Okinawa, and South Korea. Here he is greeted in Seoul (June 19, 1960).

Barbara also accompanied him on this trip.

Nixon declared his candidacy for president. Ike appears September 12, 1960, at a rally in Baltimore to kick off the campaign. *To his right:* Henry Cabot Lodge, Nixon's running mate.

Mamie votes in the 1960 election. Guess whom she voted for.

On September 22, Ike addressed the General Assembly of the United Nations primarily about emerging nations, especially the new African states. Several days thereafter, he met with many leaders of the Afro-Asian bloc such as President Gamal Abdel Nasser of Egypt.

Ike met with President-elect Kennedy
in the White House (December 6, 1960)
to prepare for the smooth and pleasant
transition.

Last Christmas in the White House. Anne was now 11; David, 12; Mary Jean, 5; and Susan, 9.

Ike's final duty as president, attending the swearing in of John F. Kennedy, January 20, 1961. *To Ike's left,* Jackie Kennedy. Behind Kennedy, Vice Presidents Lyndon Johnson and Richard Nixon.

A formal portrait of Ike after he left the White House. This is a fair representation of the president: a responsible, realistic man of high moral principle and courage, who guided the nation with dignity, wisdom, and strength.

CHAPTER 9
Afterward

**Ike enjoyed retirement and his home in
Gettysburg (January 1966).**

Retired in early 1961, Ike settled down at the Gettysburg farm that he had acquired in the Columbia days. It was from this very region that his father had emigrated as a boy with his family to Kansas. Eisenhower himself had lived here during World War I as commanding officer of Camp Colt. He was finally at home—the first home that was really his, and he was past seventy.

The farm was adjacent to the Gettysburg battlefield immortalized in American history during the bloody July days of 1863. This place became the focus of his later years with its crops and cattle and someone to manage both. There was an endless stream of visitors, politicians, and scholars as well as his own friends whom he always enjoyed entertaining. While he hoped there would be time to play bridge and catch up on reading as well as work on his paintings, he found himself busier than he had ever been. As he wrote Churchill in April, "There seems to be little cessation from the constant stream of demands upon my time and energy."

There was also business to be done, including books to be written and some systematic way of handling the visitors (the list reads like a *Who's Who*) and the pile of correspondence pouring in from all over the world. To facilitate this, he leased a two-story brick building from Gettysburg College as an office. In his status as a former president and as a general of the army (a rank that technically did not retire), he also had a staff: Robert Schultz, his long-time aide and now a brigadier general; a personal secretary; and to help in the research and writing of his memoirs, his son John, Kevin McCann, and Bill Ewald, among others.

Above all, Ike enjoyed having his family near at hand. John and Barbara had purchased an adjacent small home of their own, and it was a source of great satisfaction to Ike to have them and his four grandchildren living there. He and Mamie were close to Barbara and their grandchildren. Ike's favorite was grandson David, with whom he spent much time fishing, golfing, or just talking.

In the first four years of retirement, Ike primarily worked on the two books about his administrations *Mandate for Change* and *Waging Peace*. While his helpers sorted through a mountain of research documents, Ike would dictate his own thoughts on the topics for the memoirs. After a rough draft had been prepared, Ike returned to the task of revising and rewriting it—a long, tough process.

The books were thorough and detailed but not particularly exciting, with the second volume receiving better reviews than the first. While they are major historical contributions, little emerges from them about the central figure himself. That was reserved for a book he wrote later in retirement, *At Ease: Stories I Tell to Friends*. This informal autobiography contains material not covered in Ike's memoirs or in the earlier *Crusade in Europe*. An excellent little book, it gives insights into the man himself and is a revealing indication of the intellect, character, and ability of Eisenhower on his own, as well as his considerable charm.

For years Ike had looked forward to settling down in one place, but after all those years of moving and action, it was hard to remain full time in Gettysburg. Each winter he took a train to Palm Desert, California, where a home and office were provided by friends. The Eisenhowers also took frequent trips to Georgia, where he and Mamie stayed in "Mamie's Cottage" on the grounds of the Augusta National Golf Club. This cottage had been given to him by friends while he was still in the White House (although he did not know who they were until after he left the presidency).

Ike also took numerous business trips of various types. One of the most interesting was in August 1963, when he and Mamie went to Europe with Walter Cronkite to film "D-Day Plus 20." The film itself shows Ike driving across the Normandy beaches discussing the invasion.

Nixon's defeat in the 1960 election meant Eisenhower was still the most prominent member of the Republican party. He was greatly sought after by fellow Republicans, especially as the 1964 presidential nominations and election came along. But Ike was never comfortable with the Republican party after he left the White House; this became particularly evident in the 1964 election. In 1962 he had tried unsuccessfully to take the party leadership away from the Old Guard and the Republican National Committee. Indeed, both during and after his White House years he had toyed with the idea of forming a third party of moderate Republicans, but nothing resulted from the idea.

The problem that he and other Republicans faced in 1964 was whom to put up against Lyndon Baines Johnson. Having failed on his bid for the California governorship, Nixon was out. The frontrunners then were Senator Barry Goldwater and New York Governor Nelson Rockefeller. Not enthusiastic about either, Ike at times tried, though never forcefully, to push some candidates of his own such as Governor William Scranton of Pennsylvania. By the time of the convention, however, he conceded that Goldwater would be the candidate. The election results—a landslide for LBJ—were no surprise to the senior statesman.

Ike was a de facto consultant to the presidents who succeeded him. Both John Kennedy and Lyndon Johnson kept in touch and frequently conferred with Ike. Kennedy sought his counsel from the beginning and was particularly solicitous of his advice after the Bay of Pigs fiasco in April 1961 and during the Cuban missile crisis of October 1962. When the war in Vietnam became Johnson's main preoccupation, he relied heavily on Eisenhower.

Kennedy had first learned of Eisenhower's Cuban invasion plan shortly after the November 1960 election. Throughout the early days of his administration, JFK considered various options, including whether the force should be landed at all. In a decision that he later called "stupid," the new president finally gave the go-ahead to Operation Zapata, an invasion of Cuba by exiles. It began on Monday, April 17, 1961, and ended two days later as a complete disaster with all of the invaders either killed or captured.

On April 22, Eisenhower was back at Camp David, at Kennedy's request, to discuss the matter with the new president. Ike was particularly amazed that Kennedy had not provided air cover for the operation. JFK responded that he was trying to avoid giving away direct U.S. involvement. Eisenhower was confounded. Trained invasion brigades do not just appear out of the air. It is clear that Eisenhower would never have authorized that kind of operation despite his earlier approval of the preliminary planning and training.

Likewise, when the missile crisis came up the following October, Kennedy consulted Ike, this time *during* the crisis. Although Eisenhower played no direct part in the decision-making process, he approved of the way that Kennedy, now a more mature president, handled this dramatic confrontation with Khrushchev and the Soviet Union.

On the afternoon of November 22, 1963, Ike was attending a United Nations luncheon when word came of JFK's assassination. He flew immediately to Washington to join Kennedy's family in the East Room and stand beside the coffin. Soon after, Kennedy's vice president and successor, Lyndon Johnson, called Ike for what was to be the first of many meetings and contacts.

From the 1964 election until the spring of 1968, public life in America was dominated by Lyndon Johnson, and America was preoccupied with the war in Vietnam and how to deal with it. In early 1965 many options were open for LBJ, but by summer he had eliminated all but one—using American warriors.

At each of the war's benchmarks—the Rolling Thunder bombing campaign in the north, the troop commitment that followed, and the conduct of the war itself—Johnson consulted Eisenhower and kept him informed, sometimes by telephone, sometimes by letter, and sometimes by liaison officials. Strangely enough (or perhaps not so strangely), the man who had been very cautious about a Vietnam commitment as president was now the old soldier joining the hawks' ranks on Vietnam.

In November 1965, ten years and two months after his heart attack in Denver, Eisenhower suffered another one. After a stay in the hospital, he was back to some degree of action. Still, Ike knew what was ahead. A chapel had been built on the grounds of the Eisenhower Library and Museum in Abilene and that was where he and Mamie wanted to be buried when the time came, along with their baby Icky. Thereafter, Ike suffered a series of heart

attacks. During the last year of his life, he was a frequent patient at Walter Reed Army Hospital in Washington.

In the summer of 1968 he dropped any pretense of Republican political neutrality and, in a small news conference at the hospital, strongly endorsed Richard Nixon for the presidential nomination. In August he addressed the Republican convention from his hospital room. The next day he had another heart attack, and his health steadily declined.

On Friday morning March 28, 1969, Mamie, John, and David were with Ike in his hospital room. Looking at John, he said, "I want to go; God take me." In a few moments he was dead. Ike had returned to the heart of America.

Home at last! Ike bought a farm at Gettysburg, Pennsylvania, when he was president of Columbia University. Here the Eisenhowers returned when Ike left the presidency, and they happily spent the rest of their life in the only home they ever owned.

Retirement meant that Ike could now drive himself again. Here, for the first time in 21 years, he gets behind the wheel of a car on a hunting trip in Albany, Georgia (January 24, 1960).

Ike was now also able to spend more time at a favorite hobby—oil painting.

A painting he gave to his secretary Ann Whitman (1960).

Kennedy and Ike met at Camp David at the young president's request to discuss the Bay of Pigs disaster, for which Kennedy assumed responsibility (April 22, 1961).

When House Speaker Sam Rayburn died in November 1961, his funeral assembled Presidents Truman, Eisenhower, and Kennedy in a last tribute to the highly esteemed speaker.

Ike as seen through the five stars emblazoned on his office door in Gettysburg (June 1962).

Mamie was asked to be co-chair with Jackie Kennedy to raise funds for the new cultural center in Washington. Jackie hosted a tea for Mamie in the White House (June 22, 1962).

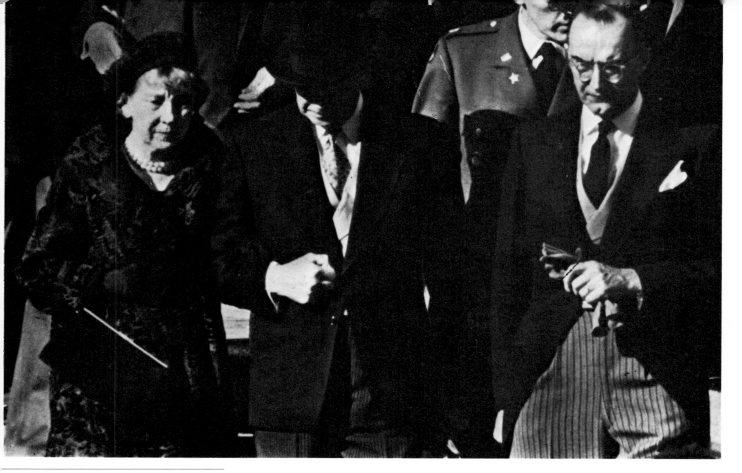

Ike and Mamie's faces reflect the shock and sadness the nation felt at the assassination of JFK. Here they leave the funeral mass for the slain president at St. Matthew's Cathedral (November 25, 1963).

The following day the new president, Lyndon Johnson, called Ike in for consultation.

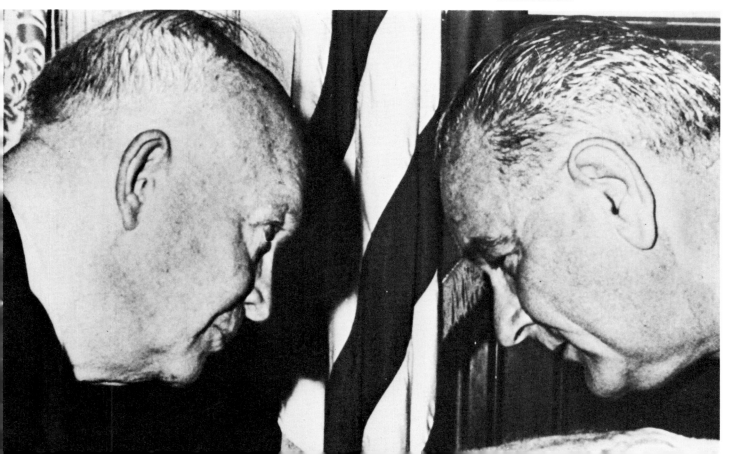

Walter Cronkite interviews Ike for
"D-Day Plus Twenty Years," a
television show on the invasion, at
Southwick House, the D-Day invasion
headquarters in England (August
1963).

Ike returns to Normandy.

ABC televised Ike discussing his White House years with a group of children sitting outside his office in Gettysburg (June 26, 1964). Ike was always greatly concerned with passing on intact the American heritage to future generations.

The Republican party looked to Ike as its senior member. Ike is at a day-long "Unity Conference" held August 12, 1964, in Hershey, Pennsylvania. *Left to right:* Governor William Scranton of Pennsylvania; Ike; Barry Goldwater, the party's standard-bearer in 1964; and Richard Nixon.

Ike professed to be "completely satisfied" with the choice of Goldwater, though he probably would have preferred the more moderate Scranton.

Ike's first book on his presidency, *Waging Peace,* was published on October 14, 1965.

In May President Johnson visited him at Walter Reed Hospital after Ike had a gall bladder operation.

Ike returns the favor. When LBJ had *his* gall bladder out, Ike visited him at Bethesda Naval Hospital, Maryland (November 1966).

On July 1, 1966, Ike and Mamie celebrated their golden wedding anniversary, and it truly had been a happy marriage of 50 years. Here they are outside their home at Gettysburg in November of that year. Retirement agreed with Ike, and for Mamie it finally meant a chance to really be with her husband instead of sharing him with the world as she had for the last quarter of a century.

General William Westmoreland, U.S. military commander in Vietnam, came home in April 1967 on a tour to promote support of the war and stopped off at Ike's Palm Desert, California, home to meet with the former president.

LBJ was another visitor to Ike's home in Palm Desert (February 1968). A memorable winter for Ike, he scored his only hole-in-one in his long golf-playing career, and he was thrilled.

Two shots of Ike conferring with President Johnson aboard Air Force One in Palm Desert.

One of the Eisenhower's happiest occasions in 1968 was the wedding of Julie Nixon and Ike's grandson David in December, but by then Ike was too ill to attend. Here Julie and David come down the aisle after the ceremony. David's hair was not cut short enough to suit Ike.

President Nixon visited Ike at Walter Reed in February just before Ike's death on March 28, 1969.

The whole world mourned his death.
French papers proclaimed, "Ike the
Liberator is dead!"

Eisenhower's coffin lay in state in Bethlehem Chapel at the Washington Cathedral, and later it was taken to the Capitol where Richard Nixon gave the elegy. It was returned to the Cathedral for the funeral, after which it was placed aboard a funeral train for the two-day ride to Abilene. He was buried on April 2, 1969.

Mamie arriving on John's arm with Barbara following behind at the Capitol Rotunda.

Mamie's anguish over the loss of her beloved Ike is clearly seen, as well as the concern of her son for his mother's travail.

Old soldier de Gaulle salutes his fallen comrade.

The flag at half staff in front of the Washington Monument on a bleak March day symbolized the nation's respect for Ike in his passing.

Ike's List of His Proudest Achievements as President

On October 18, 1966, Dwight D. Eisenhower wrote a letter to his former press secretary, James C. Hagerty, listing 23 of the proudest achievements of his eight-year presidency. The achievements were not in order of importance and were accompanied by Eisenhower's admission that "I had dashed these off the top of my head.".

★ Statehood for Alaska and Hawaii.
★ Building of St. Lawrence Seaway.
★ End of Korean War; thereafter no American killed in combat.
★ Largest reduction in taxes to that time.
★ First civil rights law in 80 years.
★ Prevention of communist efforts to dominate Iran, Guatemala, Lebanon, Formosa, South Vietnam.
★ Reorganization of the Defense Department.
★ Initiation, and the great progress in, most ambitious road program by any nation in history.
★ Slowing up and practical elimination of inflation.
★ Initiation of space program with successful orbits in less than three years, starting from scratch.
★ Initiating a strong ballistic missile program.
★ Conceiving and building the Polaris program, with ships operating at sea within a single administration.
★ Starting federal medical care for the aged (Kerr-Mills).
★ Desegregation in Washington, D.C., and armed forces even without laws.
★ Fighting for responsible fiscal and financial policies throughout eight years.
★ Extension of OASI (Old Age Survivors Insurance) to over 10 million persons.
★ Intelligent application of federal aid to education (Defense Educational Bill).
★ Preservation, for first time in American history, of adequate military establishment after cessation of war.
★ Using federal power to enforce orders of a federal court in Arkansas, with no loss of life.
★ Goodwill journeys to more than a score of nations in Europe, Asia, Africa, South America and in the Pacific.
★ Establishment of the Department of Health, Education and Welfare.
★ Initiation of plan for social progress in Latin America after obtaining necessary authorization from Congress for $500 million (later called Alliance for Progress).
★ Atoms for Peace proposal.

CHAPTER 10

Legacies

All great people leave legacies—some are tangible, some are intangible. While the former are usually recognized early, the intangible may not become clear until long after the person has merged with time. And it is often these intangible legacies that are the most important to those who are heir to them. Such is the case with Dwight Eisenhower, supreme commander in Europe during World War II and thirty-fourth president of the United States.

While his record of accomplishments as soldier and statesman is easily listed in a long and impressive litany, his influence on the lives of his countrymen today because of the tenor of his presidency, the stability of the Eisenhower era, is not yet fully realized. That stability is accepted now not so much as an accomplishment on his part but as just the way things were. The calmness of the era between Truman and Kennedy—no wars, no depressions, no wild societal swings—seems to today's adults to have been that way because nothing much happened, not because of Ike's wise and careful management of the problems and challenges that confronted him, because of the firm and courageous assertion of himself and his judgment against the easy way. The fiscal and social balance of those years came about because of Ike's leadership, not because "nothing much happened."

The Eisenhower years set the basis for the lives of those Americans now in their thirties and forties, influencing not only the quality of life of their formative years, which was taken for granted, but their expectations of the future. His policies and leadership, his personality and character had more impact on the world that formed them than any other American of that time. His was a seminal influence.

Ike and his era were different from what followed. It was the simplicity of Ike and the sturdiness of his ambience that gave the country peace, prosperity, and, yes, a little dullness. These things were subsequently scorned and thrown away in the glamour and "fun" times that followed—times of boldness and risk-taking that eventually led to social turbulence and the Vietnam War.

It is easier now to look back from a distance of 30 years and see that the man sometimes portrayed by pundits as a "do-nothing" president, well-meaning but bumbling and inarticulate, was anything but what Ike really was. That instead he was an astute, effective, courageous leader with such fundamental humility he had no need to maintain a public image or rally the masses with stirring and sometimes reckless phrases. Rather, Ike set his own course down the middle path and went forward with determination and a firm belief in the rightness of his way.

The legacy we have from Dwight David Eisenhower is more, though, than the years of peace and prosperity; it is the man himself—that there was such a person of great worth who believed in a world that was essentially good and decent and lived a life befitting it. Long after his death and shortly before her own, Mamie was asked what she would like people to remember of Ike. She answered, "His honesty. . . integrity, and admiration for mankind." Perhaps we should leave his legacies at that.

The Eisenhower Center

Commonly called the Eisenhower Center, the Dwight D. Eisenhower Presidential Library, in Abilene, Kansas, comprises five buildings: the Dwight D. Eisenhower Library, the Museum of the Presidential Library, the Family Home (see page 9), a Visitors Center, and "A Place of Meditation." It is administered by the National Archives and Records Administration, an agency of the United States Government. The public areas of the Eisenhower Center are open from 9 A.M. to 4:45 P.M. daily, including Sundays and holidays, with the exception of Thanksgiving, Christmas, and New Year's Day when they are closed.

The Dwight D. Eisenhower Library and Museum.

The Dwight D. Eisenhower Library and Museum.

The Visitors Center.

The Place of Meditation is Ike's final resting place. Also buried there are Mamie and their infant son, Icky.

Chronology of Dwight Eisenhower's Life

1890: Born David Dwight Eisenhower, in Denison, Texas, October 14. Parents: Ida and David Eisenhower.

1891: Family returns to Abilene, Kansas.

1909: Graduates from high school.

1911: Enters West Point.

1915: Graduates from West Point sixty-first in a class of 164. Commissioned second lieutenant of infantry. Assigned to Fort Sam Houston, Texas.

1916: Promoted to first lieutenant. Marries Mamie Geneva Doud in Denver, July 1.

1917: Various assignments and locations. First son Icky born September.

1918: Promoted to major (June); lieutenant colonel (October); commander, Tank Training Center, Camp Colt, Gettysburg, Pennsylvania. In 1928 receives Distinguished Service Medal for his work at Camp Colt.

1919: Command of tank units, Camp Meade, Maryland.

1920: Reduced to captain (June). Promoted to major (July).

1922: Becomes executive officer to General Fox Conner, Panama Canal Zone. Second son John born August (first son died 1921).

1925: Enters Command and General Staff School, Fort Leavenworth, Kansas.

1926: Graduates from Command and General Staff School first in his class.

1927: Assigned to American Battle Monuments Commission in Washington, D.C., to prepare guidebook on European battlefields of World War I.

1928: Graduates from Army War College in Washington, D.C.; detailed to France by Battle Monuments Commission.

1929: Returns to Washington, D.C.; becomes assistant executive in the office of Assistant Secretary of War.

1933: Assigned as assistant to General Douglas MacArthur, chief of staff, U.S. Army.

1935: Named senior assistant to General MacArthur, military adviser to the Commonwealth of the Philippines.

1936: Promoted to lieutenant colonel.

1940: Joins Fifteenth Infantry Regiment in February as executive officer, located first at Fort Ord, California, and then Fort Lewis, Washington. Chief of staff of Third Division at Fort Lewis.

1941: Chief of staff for Ninth Army Corps at Fort Lewis. Promoted to colonel. Made chief of staff for Lieutenant General Walter Krueger, commander of the Third Army at Fort Sam Houston, Texas. Promoted to brigadier general. Assigned to Washington, D.C., as assistant chief of staff, War Plans Division under General Marshall.

1942: Promoted to major general. Appointed commander of the European Theater of Operations on June 15. Promoted to lieutenant general in July. Commands Allied invasion of North Africa in November.

1943: Promoted to general. Directs invasion of Sicily in July and August. Launches Italian campaign in September. Appointed supreme commander of Allied Expeditionary Forces in December.

1944: Arrives in London in January to establish Supreme Headquarters. Directs Normandy invasion beginning June 6. Appointed general of the army in December.

1945: Accepts unconditional surrender of Germany at Reims on May 7. Makes speech at Guildhall in London on June 12. Appears before joint session of Congress on June 18. Becomes commander of United States occupation zone of Germany. Returns to Washington, D.C., as chief of staff, U.S. Army, November.

1948: Retires as chief of staff on May 2. Installed as president of Columbia University on October 12. Publishes *Crusade In Europe*.

1950: Appointed supreme commander of North Atlantic Treaty Organization, December.

1952: Announces availability as Republican candidate for president in January. Relieved as commander of North Atlantic Treaty Organization in June. Nominated for president by Republicans, July 11. Defeats Adlai E. Stevenson on November 4. Visits Korea in December.

1953: Inaugurated thirty-fourth president of the United States, January 20.

1955: Attends Geneva Summit Conference in July with British Prime Minister Anthony Eden, Marshal Nikolai Bulganin, and French Premier François Faure. Suffers heart attack in September.

1956:	Announces in February he will run for second term. Wins presidential election in November.
1959:	Visits West Germany, France, and England in support of Atlantic alliance in July. In December visits eleven Asian, European, and African countries.
1960:	Visits Philippines, Taiwan, Okinawa, and South Korea.
1961:	Retires to Gettysburg farm.
1963:	Publishes *Mandate for Change*.
1965:	Suffers two heart attacks. Publishes *Waging Peace*.
1967:	Publishes *At Ease: Stories I Tell to Friends*.
1968:	Suffers four heart attacks. Strongly endorses Richard M. Nixon for the presidency.
1969:	Dies on March 28 in Walter Reed Army Hospital, Washington, D.C., at seventy-eight.

About the Author and Photo Editor

Douglas Kinnard graduated from West Point on June 6, 1944. He was in combat in World War II in Europe, in Korea, and twice in Vietnam. The third general in his West Point class, he retired voluntarily in 1970 and joined the Princeton Department of Politics where he received a Ph.D. in 1973. His main teaching career was at the University of Vermont from which he is professor emeritus. He has published three books, including *President Eisenhower and Strategy Management*. He is now a Secretary of the Navy Senior Research Fellow at the Naval War College in Newport, Rhode Island.

Wade Tyree holds a Ph.D. in English from Princeton University. She is currently working on a book about the last great land opening in the continental United States.

Acknowledgments and Credits

Of great assistance in bringing this pictorial history together were members of the staff of the Dwight D. Eisenhower Presidential Library in Abilene, Kansas, especially Robert A. Paull, photographer, and Kathleen A. Struss and Hazel O. Stroda, archivists.

All pictures, unless otherwise credited below, are in the public realm whatever their original source, and all but a few of the photographs are in the collection of the Eisenhower Library, Abilene, Kansas.

AP/Wide World: *bottom* 40, *upper* 47, 74, *top* 82, *bottom* 91, *top* 95, *top* 96, *both* 97, *bottom 98, bottom* 100, *top left* 101, *bottom* 103, *bottom* 111, *both* 115, *bottom* 132, *bottom* 139, *bottom* 144, *bottom* 149, *bottom right* 150, *top left* 152, *bottom* 153, *top* 155, *top* 160, *top* 161, *bottom* 163, *bottom* 164, *bottom* 165, *bottom 170, top* 172.

U.S. Army: *top* 15, *bottom* 21, *bottom right* 23, *bottom left* 27, *all* 28, *bottom* 30, *top* 32, *bottom* 34, *bottom* 35, 37, *both* 41, *top* 42, *bottom right* 44, *both* 46, *bottom left and right* 47, *top* 48, 51 *and top center* 54, *top and bottom left* 54, *bottom right* 55, *top* 57, *bottom right* 57, 58, *all* 59, *bottom* 60, *all* 61, *both* 62, *both* 63, *top* 64, 65, *both* 66, *both* 67, *both* 68, *top and bottom left* 69, *both* 71, *both* 72, *bottom* 80, *bottom* 92, *top* 93, *bottom* 104, *top* 105, 110, *top* 112, *top* 143, 157, *bottom* 171, *bottom* 172.

C.S. Borjes: *bottom* 82.

© **1962 Capital Cities/ABC, Inc.:** *top right* 165.

Copyrighted, Chicago Tribune Company, all rights reserved, used with permission: *top right* 101.

U.S. Coast Guard: *top and bottom spreads* 54–55, *bottom* 56.

Red Grandy, *Stars & Stripes*: *top* 90.

from HERBLOCK'S SPECIAL FOR TODAY. (Simon & Schuster, 1958): *top* 120, *top* 123, *bottom* 137.

I.H.T. Corporation. Reprinted by Permission: *top* 85, *top* 87, *bottom* 96, *middle* 153, *top* 163, *top* 166.

Imperial War Museum, London: *top right* 55, *top left and right* 56.

Keystone Press Agency: *top* 40.

National Park Service: *bottom right* 32, 109, *top* 114, *top* 117, *top* 121, *bottom* 125, 129, *top* 141, *top* 142, *top* 153, 154.

U.S. Navy: *bottom* 135, *bottom* 136, *top* 140, 145, 146, *top right* 150, *bottom left* 151, *bottom* 160, *bottom* 162.

Republic of China: *bottom* 152.

Republican National Committee: *top* 98, *middle* 124.

Mr. Alan W. Richards: 75.

Abbie Rowe. Courtesy National Park Service: *bottom* 29.

SHAPE: *top* 91, *top* 137.

U.S. Army Signal Corps: 83.

George Tames: 107.

UPI/Bettmann Archive: *top* 9, *top* 13, *top* 30, *both* 45, 50, *both* 70, 73, 77, *top* 78, *top* 84, *bottom* 86, *top* 89, *bottom* 90, *top* 92, *bottom* 93, *top left and right* 94, *bottom* 101, *bottom* 102, 106, *bottom* 113, *bottom* 117, *both* 118, *both* 119, *bottom* 121, 122, *bottom* 123, *top* 125, 126, 127, *both* 130, *both* 131, *top* 135, *both* 138, *bottom* 140, *bottom* 141, *bottom* 142, *bottom* 143, *top* 144, *top right* 152, *top* 161, *top* 162, *top left* 165, *bottom* 167.

USIA: *bottom* 88.

Ted T. Varner (retired), Weirton Steel Corporation: *bottom left* 99.

J. Anthony Wills: 156.

Richard Winburn: *top* 169.